Unearthing Hidden Jewels

First Edition
(1436 AH/2015 AC)

Copyright © 1436 AH/2015 AC
amana publications
10710 Tucker Street
Beltsville, MD 20705-2223 USA
Tel. 301.595.5777
Fax 301.595.5888
Email: amana@amana-corp.com
www.amanapublications.com

Cover:
Entrance of SABA' MASJID, Madina
at the site of Ghazwah al-Khandaq, the Battle of Trench
Photo credit: Zoheb Munshi

Library of Congress Cataloging-in-Publication Data

Poisson, Loretta, author.
  Unearthing hidden jewels : captivating stories of companions of the Prophet of Arabia / Loretta J. Poisson ; illustrations by Tesneem Madani.
      pages cm
   ISBN 978-1-59008-082-5
   1. Muhammad, Prophet, -632--Companions--Anecdotes. I. Madani, Tesneem, illustrator. II. Title.
   BP75.5.P65 2015
   297.6'48--dc23
                                    2015032871

Printed in the United States of America

Unearthing Hidden Jewels

CAPTIVATING STORIES OF COMPANIONS OF THE PROPHET OF ARABIA

Loretta J. Poisson

Illustrations by Tesneem Madani

amana publications

The Jewels...

Courage

The Unstoppable Soul	2
A Rare Hue of Courage	7
The Dignity of Courage	12
The Embodiment of Graceful Courage	18

- Al Baraa' b. Malik al Ansari • Abdullah bin Umm Maktum
- Abdullah b. Hudhafah as-Sahmi • Khawlah bint Al-Azwar

Asceticism

The Bounty of Asceticism	25
The Jewel of Asceticism	32
The Futility of Wealth	39
The Offerings of a Heart in Flower	44

- Al Abu Dharr Al-Ghifari • Sa'id bin 'Amir Al-Jamahi
- Suhaib Rumi • Aisha bint Abu Bakr

Loyalty

The Unwavering Promise	50
True of Heart, Noble of Deed	56
Safeguarding the *Deen*	63
The Dawn of Islam	70

- Thumamah bin Uthal • Abu 'Ubaydah bin Al-Jarrah
- Hamza ibn 'Abd al-Muttalib • Khadijah bint Khuwaylid

Sacrifice

Surrender of Desires	77
The Well of Good	84
Unearthing the Cherished Core	90
An Unyielding Tenacity	96

- Jafar ibn AbuTalib • Amr ibn Al-Jamuh
- Mus'ab ibn Umar • Nusaibah bint K'ab

FORBEARANCE

The Fortified Heart 103
The Unflappable Soul 110
The Enduring Soul 117
A Heart Reined In 123

- Bilal ibn Rabah • Zayd al-Khairi
- Abu Hurairah • Umm Salamah

COMMITMENT

Adherence to a Vow 130
The Deeply Obliging Heart 139
The Duty of a Heart to its Soul 145
Two Hearts and a Shared Covenant 152

- Salman Farsi • Abu Ayyub • At-Tufayl bin 'Amr Ad-Dawsi
- Fatima bint Mohammad

GENEROSITY

A Rich and Lilting Endowment 158
The Eternal Harvest 165
The Selfless Outpouring 172
The Heart that Mends 177

- Abdullah bin Mas'ud • 'Akrimah bin Abu Jahl
- Abdurrahman bin Auf • Rufaidah Aslamiyyah

OBEDIENCE

The Amenable Soul 181
The Abiding Heart 187
The Soul that Heeds 192
The Offering of an Heir 199

- Abdullah bin Jahsh • Said bin Zaid • Sa'ad Ibn Abi Waqqas
- Umm Sulaym bint Milhan Al-Ansariyyah

Did You Know...
The Golden Age of Islam and Beyond

The Prophet's sword - words of peace on a weapon of war 6

Hajj Ali comes to America 10

Before Columbus – Muslims in America 17

Zubaidah bint Jaf'ar's waterway to Makkah 23

Abu al-Qasim Khalaf ibn Abbas al-Zahrawi – father of modern surgery ... 30

Ibn Haitham and the camera 37

English words – Arabic roots 43

Ibn Battuta, traveler of the known world 48

Tibet and Islam 55

Al-Jazari - the father of modern robotics 61

The Chicago World's Fair of 1893 – a touch of Islam in America 68

Abbas ibn Firnas of Andalucía took flight 82

Harun al-Rashid and the House of Wisdom 88

Short history of the 'ud 94

Astrolabes were ancient global positioning instruments 102

Who are the Melungeons? 108

The legend of coffee 115

Ziryab and the civilizing of civilization 121

Shajarat al Durr, the "other" queen of Egypt 128

Ibn Sina and his "Canon of Medicine" 138

The Golden Age and the Renaissance 143

To Timbuktu and back 150

Al Udar al Karima, ruler of Yemen 157

Zheng He, Admiral of the Chinese Navy 163

Al-Kindi, pigeons, and the cracking of codes 170

Al-Idrisi and the first World Atlas 176

Major hospitals in the Muslim world 180

The destruction of the House of Wisdom – Hulagu's revenge 185

The path to papermaking 191

Gunpowder, Al Rammah, and ingenious war devices 197

Builder of the world's oldest active university - Fatima al Fihri 204

Preface

Who doesn't love a great action movie with its noble causes, good and evil, bravery and loyalty? But when I saw 'The Lord of the Rings' it touched a deep part of me rarely reached. I watched in wonder as the good guys, with absolute certainty, plunged headlong into a throng of purely venomous creatures. Against insurmountable odds, they were willing to give up life and limb for their belief that there was good in the world worth fighting for. "How could they do it?" I wondered. What strength of heart gave them the ability to face such wickedness? It was fascinating! A little while later I came across a very old series of paperback books (some held together with oversized staples) about the companions, and as I began to read, I realized that the beginnings of Islam were exactly like this, and more. Any story put out by Hollywood paled in comparison to the stories of the men and women that surrounded our Prophet (peace be upon him). They were brave, loyal, steadfast, loving, determined, and faced even greater evil than the creatures in these movies. As you open up the pages of this book, put yourself there, in Arabia, and see if you don't share their struggle for goodness. Find that part of you rarely touched and read on as the past unfolds before your eyes in full-spectrum colors of tenacity and fortitude.

Enjoy!

– Loretta J. Poisson

Introduction

The life of the Prophet (pbuh) is not the only source of guidance from the prophetic times. What about the converts to Islam after revelation began? The lessons in their search for truth are our lessons. Their struggles are directly relevant to the resistance we meet today. Their victories are the bedrock on which we build our enriching way of life.

What are the ingredients for a just society?

Courage overcomes resistance, Asceticism diffuses the lifetime, Loyalty is the enclosure that makes it sturdy, Sacrifice allows "give and take", Forbearance gives an ear to the voices, Commitment keeps any from turning back, Generosity levels out the curves of wealth, and Obedience unifies.

The character of these honorable men and women comprised the soul of Islam, propelling it forward. Their stirring adventures gave life to a movement destined for greatness. Their deeds urged the effusive spread of Islam like life-giving rains flowing across barren land.

Their commitment and sacrifice never allowed the fire to go out of the hearts and minds of those who witnessed their steadfast obedience.

Armed with the knowledge of our pious predecessors, hope lies in remembrance of what was…

Courage–The Unstoppable Soul

"Indeed, Allah has purchased from the believers their lives and their properties; in exchange for that they will have Paradise. They fight in the cause of Allah, so they slay and are slain. It is a true promise binding upon Him in the Torah and the Gospel and the Qur'an. And who is truer to His covenant than Allah? So rejoice in the bargain which you have made, and this is the great attainment." {The Qur'an, 9:111}

What moves a man's heart to ride into the heat of battle, while all around him wafts the smell of conquered souls, razor-sharp sabers only a hair's breath from connecting – yet, he wades in…firm of heart, fear left abandoned, not a part of provisions packed. Does he believe his life is worthless? No, on the contrary, he feels a richness to it, a gift he wishes to give to his Lord on High.

The *Oxford American Dictionary* defines 'courage' as: (1) the ability to control fear when facing danger or pain. (2) Bravery (3) To be brave enough to do what one feels to be right.

Muslims define 'courage' as Al Baraa' b. Malik, and here is his story…

Al Baraa' b. Malik al Ansari

Quote: *"A man's measure is his will."* –Ali ibn Abu Talib

Umar bin Khattab sent letters to the governors in his provinces saying, "Do not make al-Baraa' the head of any Muslim army; his enthusiasm may lead to their deaths."

This small-framed man with disheveled hair, Al Baraa' b. Malik, appeared to be one that a person would hardly give a second glance to, but he single-handedly defeated over a hundred non-believers in duels, and this did not include all those he had vanquished in battles.

Musaylamah the Liar, a false prophet who had claimed his prophethood in the time of the Prophet (pbuh), came to the forefront after the death of our beloved Prophet (pbuh), and he was from the tribe of Banu Hanifa. He was able to gather a band of seasoned warriors who followed him because of solid and enduring tribal affiliations. The Battle of Yamamah was fought against those who left Madina after the Prophet died, swearing they didn't need to pay the *Zakat* on their wealth anymore and joining the false prophet, Musaylimah, who only wanted land and power. Musaylimah had insulted the Prophet (pbuh), set people against the Muslims, and tortured the believers whenever they dared to venture close to his lands.

The first Muslim forces sent to deal with Musaylamah were defeated and soundly routed by the renegades, and so another group of Muslims, led by Khalid bin Al-Walid, went forth. Al-Baraa' b. Malik was among this force along with many prominent Companions. As the conflict raged on the battlefield, Musaylamah and his group gained the upper hand, and the Believers were badly shaken. They retreated until the enemy forces were able to breach the encampment of Khalid ibn Walid, where, if not for the protection of one of his adversaries, Khalid's wife would have been killed.

The Muslims knew the situation was dire, and losing this crucial battle could mean a major setback for the cause of Islam, as well as all of the Muslims on the Arabian Peninsula. The heroic stories are many, but this is a sample of how some of the believers stepped up to gain victory:

Thabit b. Qays, standard bearer for the Ansar, rubbed his body with embalming spices, adorned himself with his shroud, and dug a shallow trench. After much enemy bloodshed, this is the spot where he died for the cause of Islam.

Zayd b. Al-Khattab, brother of Umar (radiAllahu anhu), rushed forth, calling out to his companions, "Grit your teeth, strike the enemy, and move forward. I am taking a vow of silence, and will not speak until Musaylamah is defeated, or I meet my Maker and tell Him that I died trying!" This stance brought him martyrdom.

Salim, the freedman of Abu Hudhayfah, carried the banner of those who had migrated for Allah's sake, and when they feared for his safety and theirs because of his fatigue, he cried out, "If you are attacked, then I am not worthy to live on as a Preserver of the Qur'an!" He persevered until he was wounded and carried off the battlefield.

As the fighting reached its boiling point, Khalid bin Al-Walid ordered Al-Baraa' to, "Lead the assault on them, Oh, Knight of the Ansar!"

Al-Baraa' turned to his troops and cried out, "Onward, Ansar! Let not any of you think that you may return to our beloved city, Al-Madina. You have no place to go home to. There is only Allah, and Paradise!"

The energized core of Muslims charged in, and with Al-Baraa's sword felling many of the enemy, the tide began to turn for the fighters in the way of Allah.

The disbelievers took refuge in the "Orchard of Death", being called that later for the great number of people who were slain there. This orchard had high walls, and the entrance was bolted. The Muslims were rained down upon from above with arrows, and Al-Baraa' shouted, "Quickly, turn over a shield and I will climb on it, then raise it with your lances and toss me over the wall near the gate. I will open the gates for you, or die as a martyr in the process!" They lay a shield flat for him, and his diminutive body slid on, and was raised by dozens of lances and tossed over the wall. Like a thunderbolt, he descended on the enemy, killing many of them to clear a path to open the gate. The Muslims poured in, and, at the same time, still more scaled the walls, slaying the treacherous enemy by the thousands until they reached Musaylamah, and finally killed this imposter.

Al-Baraa' did not get his wish that day to be a martyr, but over eighty sword and arrow wounds were inflicted on his war-ravaged body. Khalid bin Al-Walid stayed with him for a month or more, until Allah restored his health to him. This unstoppable man proves that the human spirit, when well directed, is unrivaled in its capacity to overcome evil.

~~~

From the characteristics of the Companions was their firm trusting of their affairs to Allah. They would never seek anything for themselves without there being a connection with Allah (Subhanahu Wa Ta'ala). Allah said in the Qur'an, 3:173-174: "Those to whom hypocrites said, 'Indeed, the people have gathered against you, so fear them.' But it merely increased them in faith, and they said, 'Sufficient for us is Allah, and He is the best Disposer of affairs.'"

Bringing it forward to today

Were there times in your life where you wanted to have the courage to speak the truth, to enjoin good and forbid evil, and push yourself to the height of belief in Allah and Islam? Every day is full of choices and the role model of Al-Baraa' b. Malik is as relevant today as on the field of Yamamah. Every cell of his body was intent on goodness and victory for his Lord's religion, and one wonders how a heart the size of the sky could be held in such a tiny body. Let us try to move forward with more courage, Islamic dignity, and determination to do right in our short lives here on earth.

Inscribed on the hilt of the Prophet Muhammad's sword was:

"Forgive him who wrongs you; join him who cuts you off; do good to him who does evil to you, and speak the truth, although it be against yourself."

A Rare Hue of Courage

"The Prophet frowned and turned away, because there came to him the blind man, interrupting. But what would make you perceive, [O Muhammad], that perhaps he might be purified, or be reminded, and the remembrance would benefit him? As for he who thinks himself without need, to him you give attention. And not upon you is any blame if he will not be purified. But as for he who came to you striving for knowledge, while he fears Allah, from him you are distracted. No! Indeed, these verses are a reminder..." {The Qur'an, 80:1-11}

Imagine a stone in the midst of a raging river, how it splits the torrent in two, never giving up, never faltering, facing forward, a citadel of resolve in a sea of turmoil.

Now, close your eyes and enter the world of Ibn Umm Maktum. His hearing, made acute by the endless night he was born into, was aware of the sounds of war moving past him as he remained steadfast in the tempest. Swords sparked, vanquished souls screamed, and the odor of death wafted around him, yet he stood steady, unmoving, a symbol of faith shining like armor protecting and making safe, keeping firm all who witnessed his resolute valor. An unwavering stone in a surging river of strive. Ahh, how sweet is the soul of conviction.

Quote: *"Glory be to the One who showed some of His slaves His Paradise before they met Him, and opened its gates to them when they were still in this world of deeds and actions, so some of its breezes and fragrance came to them, which made them devote their energy to seeking it and competing in attaining it."* –Ali ibn Abu Talib

ABDULLAH BIN UMM MAKTUM

No one could have known how tenaciously this sightless child would clamor to compete for Allah's pleasure and the life to come.

Abdullah bin Umm Maktum was a Makkan from the tribe of Quraish, and the first cousin of our beloved Khadijah, wife of our Prophet (pbuh).

He was one of the earliest to declare Islam, and was persecuted severely by his own people for it.

This pressure only increased his faith and devotion to Allah and His Messenger (pbuh). He never passed up a chance to be taught by the Prophet (pbuh) and this was how the verses came down regarding his zeal for knowledge. One day, he came to the Prophet (pbuh) when the Prophet (pbuh) was engaged in a conversation about Islam with the leaders of Quraish, and Ibn Umm Maktum asked him to "teach me what Allah has taught you." But the Blessed Prophet frowned and turned away. He (pbuh) was intent on strengthening the Muslim community through a tribal alliance, and wanted to finish his discussion with the Quraish. On the Prophet's (pbuh) way home, Allah sent down the first sixteen verses of *Surah 'Abasa* quoted in the beginning of this section. From then on, the Prophet (pbuh) attended to Ibn Umm Maktum's needs, and whenever he saw him coming, he would say, "Welcome to the one for whose sake my Lord admonished me."

Ibn Umm Maktum was the first of the honored Muslim's sent to Yathrib, later called Madina, to teach the people there about the Qur'an, and his first converts there were the ones who eventually invited the Prophet (pbuh) to come and live in their city. After hijrah, Ibn Umm Maktum became one who used his voice to call to prayer, making sure all were beckoned to that which gave them life.

This devoted companion was so well thought of by the Prophet (pbuh) that he was left in charge of the governing of Madina when the Prophet (pbuh) needed to travel.

The second time a revelation was sent down on his bequest was regarding *jihad*. Allah (swt) sent down the verses saying that those who went on *jihad* had a higher rank than those who stayed behind, so Ibn Umm Maktum made a supplication asking Allah to reveal that he was excused because of his blindness. Allah granted him this, and the verse came down saying, "…the believers who stay behind and who have no handicap." {The Qur'an: 48:17}

Even though this devoted companion had his excuse, his virtuous heart could not rest…it longed to prove itself in *jihad*. He decided that he would not miss a battle from then on, and his role would be that of "keeper of the banner". He used to say, "I will hold the banner of Islam, and keep it in the ranks, for I am blind, and unable to run away."

In the fourteenth year of hijrah, Umar (ra) wanted to engage the Persians in their own country, and he put out the call for any able-bodied Muslims to come and fight. One of those who answered the call was Ibn Umm Maktum. He came forth wearing a vest of armor and brandishing a full set of weapons. He took the banner and swore to protect it to the death. For three days the armies fiercely crossed swords, until finally Allah gave victory to the Muslims, but at the cost of many martyrs, one of whom was Ibn Umm Maktum. He was found on the field covered with blood, clutching the beloved banner of Islam to his chest.

"Welcome to Paradise, oh, you of cloudless inner sight!"

Unearthing Hidden Jewels

~~~

From the characteristics of the Companions was their unconcern for worldly gains and their intense and focused struggle for the Hereafter. They constantly strove to make preparations for the Afterlife.

One of them said, "If it can be that no one beats you to Allah, then do so."

Another said, "If you see someone competing to overtake you in worldly things, then compete to overtake him in the matters of *deen*."

BRINGING IT FORWARD TO TODAY

How does having sight keep us from doing good deeds? Are we afraid that someone might see us if we give money to the poor on the street? How do TV, Internet, and video games, all of which fill our eyes with the *haram*, keep us safe and on the straight path? Your eyes are a gift to be used for good. Let them see the best of everything.

Did You Know?

A Muslim named Hajj Ali came to America from Western Turkey in the 19th century with a load of camels, 33 in all, purchased by the U.S. army for use in the deserts of the Southwestern United States. Another shipment of 41 camels and six camel herders came later. The 'camel experiment' failed because the camels spooked the mules and horses around them and the owners of these skittish animals shot and killed those camels. Ali freed the last camel in 1868, and legend has it that he went out into the desert and breathed his last with his arm around a dead camel. In 1938, the Arizona Highway Department erected a monument over Ali's grave topped with a copper camel.

Many years later there were two films made about Hajj Ali, one was a highly fictionalized comedy made in the halls of Hollywood called "*Hawmps*." This was not really a fitting tribute to such an interesting life lived. The other was a drama called, "*Southwest Passage*".

Unearthing Hidden Jewels

THE DIGNITY OF COURAGE

"You will not find a people who believe in Allah and the Last Day having affection for those who oppose Allah and His Messenger, even if they were their fathers or their sons or their brothers or their kindred. Those – He has decreed within their hearts faith and supported them with spirit from Him."
{The Qur'an, 58:22}

What compels the sailboat to cut through the sea like a surgeon's knife, gliding freely from wave to wave, as if slithering on ice? It is in need of that ruffling breeze, puffing the sails out, making them ready to accept the insistent advice whispered to them to veer right or left, the breeze shepherding the craft, oh-so-confidently, to its fated end.

Then what is steadfastness, but the courage to keep oneself in position to receive the wind that guides; its maneuvering always steady, resolute, and unyielding. Gently and deftly does our Lord keep us on course.

The unswerving devotion of the next companion should be an inspiration to all those desirous of their Lord's good pleasure.

ABDULLAH B. HUDHAFAH AS-SAHMI

Quote: "*Forbearance is the root of quietness and assurance forever.*""

In the sixth year of the hijrah, the Prophet (pbuh) sent a group of his companions as emissaries to the rulers of neighboring empires, their purpose being to call these rulers to Islam. The danger was great, as these messengers would be going alone to distant lands, unfamiliar, with no way to know the language or the nature of the rulers. Yet, they were to call these rulers to leave their old beliefs and forsake their power and position to enter into the religion of Islam. This task was so perilous that anyone who chose to undertake this journey got his affairs in order before he left. The Prophet (pbuh) chose Abdullah b. Hudhafah to be his representative to Persia. He was to invite Khusraw, the ruthless Sasanian emperor into the fold of Islam.

Abdullah bade goodbye to his wife and children for what he thought might be the last time, and with no companion but Allah, traveled the unadorned path to Persia.

He announced himself when he arrived, and the emperor decorated the hall in his honor, and ordered the notables of Persia to attend the court and witness the meeting with him. Abdullah b. Hudhafah entered Khusraw's court with his head held up, his soul filled with belief, the might of Islam deep within his heart; any pride he was feeling was coming from his love of Allah and His Messenger (pbuh). Khusraw signaled for one of his courtiers to take the letter from Abdullah, but Abdullah said, "No, the Blessed Prophet (pbuh) ordered me to give it to you by hand, and I would never disobey any order of the Blessed Prophet."

The Emperor then waved his courtier aside and Abdullah stepped forward.

Once the letter was delivered, an Arab scribe from Al-Hirah read its contents:

"In the name of Allah, Most Gracious, Most Merciful, from Muhammad, the Messenger of Allah to Khusraw, Emperor of Persia. Peace be upon him who follows the Divine guidance…"

When Khusraw heard this greeting, he was filled with rage, for the Prophet (pbuh) had begun with his own name instead of putting the emperor first. He grabbed the scroll and tore it to bits, claiming, "He thus addresses me, when he is my slave?" He then told Abdullah to leave, and as Abdullah left the court he wondered what would become of him now; would he be killed or set free. He gathered himself then and exclaimed, "I swear by Allah, I care not what happens to me, as long as I have delivered the message of Allah's Messenger." He jumped on his mount, riding off as fast as he could, coaxing his camel to run with all speed.

The emperor's men pursued, but Abdullah's camel outran them. When the Prophet (pbuh) heard what Khusraw had done with the letter, he made a simple supplication, "May Allah tear apart his dominion."

This was answered when, a short time later, Khusraw's son killed him, taking his father's place on the throne of Persia.

The other half of this tale takes place in the nineteenth year after hijrah when Umar b. Al-Khattab sent an army to do battle with the Byzantines, and one of the soldiers was Abdullah b. Hudhafah As-Sahmi. Heraclius, the emperor of Byzantium was curious about the stories he heard of these Muslim soldiers and their sincere faith and sacrifice. He ordered that any Muslim captives be kept alive and brought to him. It was Allah's Will that Abdullah should be one of those captured, and when Heraclius was told that Abdullah had been one of the companions of the Prophet (pbuh), he looked this prisoner over and said, "I wish to make you an offer. If you accept to become Christian, I will set you free and be generous with you as well."

Abdullah answered with, "Far be it from me. Death is a thousand times more preferable to me than an offer such as the one you make."

The emperor tried again, saying, "I see that you are a chivalrous man, so if you accept my offer, I will bestow on you a share in my power and position."

Wrapped in his chains, the captive smiled and said, "If you were to give me all that you own, and all that the Arabs own, I still would not leave the religion of Muhammad for a second!"

"Then," the emperor replied, "I will have you killed."

"Do as you wish," was the quick response of the companion of the Prophet (pbuh).

They tortured and crucified him and shot arrows at his arms and legs as he was bound, but he refused to give up Islam. Heraclius then ordered him taken down, and he had a huge caldron filled with boiling oil brought forth, and threw two of Abdullah's companions in it. As their skin dissolved from the searing liquid, the Emperor again made the offer for Abdullah to become Christian, and he again refused.

The emperor then ordered Abdullah to be thrown into the caldron, and as he was being led to the boiling pot, tears came to his eyes, and the emperor's men informed the ruler of this. Thinking Abdullah wept in fear, Heraclius ordered him to be brought back to him and gave him a final chance to give up Islam. When Abdullah refused, Heraclius said, "May you perish! Why, then, were you weeping?"

Abdullah stood to his full height and said, "I wept when I realized I would die, and would have only one soul to sacrifice and achieve

Allah's pleasure. Would that I had as many souls to sacrifice as I have hairs on my head. I would gladly have them all thrown in the cauldron."

Exasperated, the tyrant said, "If I set you free, will you kiss my head?"

Now feeling in the position to bargain, Abdullah said, "Only if you free all the other Muslim captives."

"So be it," was the response.

Abdullah came forward and kissed the head of the emperor, and all prisoners were set free. When Abdullah got back and reported what had happened to Umar (ra), Umar said, "Every Muslim should kiss the head of Abdullah b. Hudhafah, and I shall be the first one to do it," and he rose and kissed him on the head. Humble was the one who kissed, and humbled was the one who received this kiss…

~~~

From the characteristics of the Companions was their magnifying of the rights of Muslim sanctity, wanting and loving for their fellow Muslims all good.

The Messenger of Allah (pbuh) said, "A Muslim is sacred to another Muslim, his blood, wealth, and honor."

Abdullah bin 'Abbas (ra) said, "The best deed is generosity towards one with whom he sits."

Bringing it Forward to Today

In today's world, the rich and famous are revered, and many times, there is not a shred of belief in these people's hearts. We need to be looking to the righteous, and benefitting from their knowledge and purity, keeping company with them as much as possible. This will, God willing, give us the conviction of faith that will help us weather the storms that blow an ill wind past our hearts.

Did You Know?

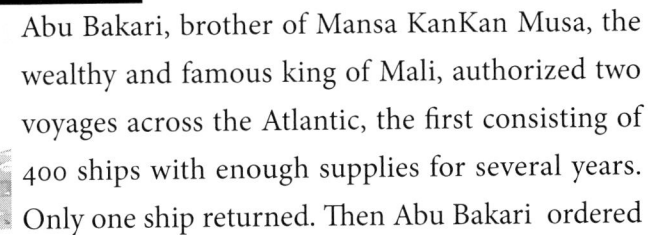

Abu Bakari, brother of Mansa KanKan Musa, the wealthy and famous king of Mali, authorized two voyages across the Atlantic, the first consisting of 400 ships with enough supplies for several years. Only one ship returned. Then Abu Bakari ordered 2,000 ships to sail, some ships carrying African Elephants, and these ships sailed in either 1307 or 1311 (this was more than a hundred years before Columbus!). These heavily-laden ships never returned. Later, there were Mandinka inscriptions found in Brazil, Peru, and the US, meaning that the voyage was successful. The travelers left religious inscriptions in the Mandinka language referring to the purpose of man to worship God, to mature, and eventually die. They intermarried with the Carib Indians in the Carribean islands. There were Mandinka inscriptions found along the Mississippi river all the way to Arizona, which means they used the Mississippi to explore northwards through the US and Canada. A fascinating inscription in a cave in the city of Four Corners, Arizona describes the heat of the desert and notes that this heat made many elephants sick and angry.

EMBODIMENT OF GRACEFUL COURAGE

"Not equal are those believers remaining at home - other than the disabled - and those who strive and fight in the cause of Allah with their wealth and their lives. Allah has preferred a higher rank for the mujahedeen through their wealth and their lives over those who remain behind." {The Qur'an, 4:95}

How is feminine defined? Is it called weakness, or is it softness with courage. Is it nurturing, or a heart big enough to hold an *ummah*. Is it called tender, or just knowing when to pull back and listen. Strength has many layers, and men wear it like a coat of armor, letting it shield and protect them, but women pull it from within, from a deep knowing of pain and sorrow, something unshakable.

Muslim women rejoice in the fortitude of this undaunted companion.

KHAWLAH BINT AL-AZWAR

Quote: *"Do not use your energy except for a cause more noble than yourself. Such a cause cannot be found except in Almighty God Himself: to preach the truth, to defend womanhood, to repel humiliation which your Creator has not imposed upon you, to help the oppressed. Anyone who uses his energy for the sake of the vanities of the world is like someone who exchanges gemstones for gravel. There is no nobility in anyone who lacks faith. The wise man knows that the only fitting price for his soul is a place in Paradise..."* –Ibn Hazm

Khawlah bint Al-Azwar was the daughter of a chief of Bani Asad, and this brave and intelligent family converted to Islam in the early years. Dirar was the beloved brother of Khawlah, and was a knight in his own right, wise, renowned for his fearlessness and poetic fluidity. He would fight with no armor, wading into the midst of the enemy in full fighting mode. His love for his sister was legendary, and they were trained together in swordsmanship and strategies of battle. He continued his training of Khawlah, as he himself became a master of the art of fighting in impossible situations.

Khawlah was tall and slim, with great beauty, and she was also excellent in poetry. They would go to battle together, and she would carry water and help the wounded while he was in the thick of hostilities.

In the war against the Byzantines, these siblings were together at the battle of Ajnadin near Jerusalem. In the heat of the battle, Dirar went forward into a large company of Romans and slashed his way to the Emperor Heraclius's son. He killed him along with many others. With great effort, the enemy finally subdued him and captured him. Word came to Khawlah that her brother had been either killed or captured, no one knew which. She did what he had trained her to do; she put on her black armor, green turban, and a face veil to conceal her identity. At that time, men and women both wore this on the desert to keep out the sand. She began frantically looking for him, using much the same tactics of wading in and killing as many as she could and then pushing out the other side, only to turn around and go in again, taking many casualties as she searched.

The Muslim army then started to notice this "Knight" and his bravery and recklessness, and they wondered who it might be. At first they all thought it was Khalid ibn Walid, but when he came riding up to them to ask them who this knight was, they said, "We thought it was you!" Khalid saw from afar a tall Muslim knight, dressed in black, his nose and mouth covered, with a green turban wrapped around his helmet. He said, "We need to save this man and have him fight with us. "He is a master of the art of horsemanship, encirclement, and enclosure; he charges the enemy as if he were fire. I am impressed by the excellent skills he has shown."

They could see that the Romans were shaken by his ferocity, and the Muslims wanted this Knight to fight on their side. The Knight kept exposing himself to certain death, but came out unharmed. He showed no care for himself. He let parties of Roman knights follow him; then turned upon them and routed them. The black knight disappeared among the Romans, and then reappeared with his lance dripping with blood. The Black Knight could not be overtaken. He fought alone.

Khalid exclaimed, "Oh, Assembly of Muslims! Attack all of you together. Come to the aid of this Defender of God's faith."

The Black Knight saw them coming and started to run, so they followed and surrounded her, but she was trying to conceal her identity, so she made a turn and escaped. They kept after her, trying to find out which tribe 'he' belonged to so they could have bragging rights. Khalid pursued her until she got tired and stopped. He rode up next to her and said, "Why did you not follow my command to stop?"

He was shocked when a female voice came out from the veil.

"I didn't want to embarrass you, Oh, Amir of the righteous warriors."

When Khalid got over his surprise, he asked her why she was fighting.

"I am Dirar's sister, and I am searching for my beloved brother," was her quick reply.

Khalid understood then and encouraged her thus, "We will attack together, and place our hope in Allah that he will bring us to your brother."

They moved into formation with Khawlah in the lead. When the Romans saw the Black Knight united with the Muslims, their fear of the relentless fighter got the best of them and the Muslims easily routed them and were victorious.

Khawlah then went man to man to find some news of Dirar, but when she heard nothing of him, she began to grieve, and in between her weeping was heard, "O MY MOTHER'S SON, IF ONLY I KNEW IN WHICH DESERT THEY HAVE THROWN YOUR BODY OR WHOSE SPEAR HEADS HAVE STABBED YOU OR WHOSE SWORD HAS KILLED YOU. O MY BROTHER, YOUR SISTER IS HERE AS YOUR SACRIFICE. IF ONLY I COULD SEE YOU AGAIN, I WOULD DELIVER YOU FROM YOUR ENEMIES' HANDS. IF ONLY I KNEW IF I WILL EVER SEE YOU AGAIN AFTER THIS DAY. SON OF MY MOTHER, YOU HAVE LEFT IN YOUR SISTER'S HEART A HOT COAL AND ITS FLAME WILL NEVER BE QUENCHED. HAVE YOU JOINED OUR FATHER WHO WAS KILLED WITH THE PROPHET? IF SO, THEN PEACE BE UPON YOU, UNTIL THE LAST DAY'S MEETING."

By the time she finished, everyone around her was in tears.

The next day, their attacks on the Byzantines were even fiercer until the enemy surrendered, and Khawlah again frantically searched for news of her brother. Finally, a group of Roman men said, "You mean the one who fights without armor, the one who killed many to get to the Emperor's son?"

"Yes," she exclaimed, "That is him!"

They relayed to her that he had been taken prisoner and was sent with one hundred Knights to Constantinople by way of Homs. Khawlah immediately began pulling on her armor and grabbed her weapons, mounting her horse for the journey. Khalid had already formed a rescue party of Raafi' b 'Umairah and a hundred of his best knights.. Khalid said to Raafi', "You know her courage; you have seen her fight; take her with you." Raafi' simply said, "I hear and I obey."

Khawlah used her formidable skills as a tracker, and when she found that the trail went cold past a certain point she remarked, "Good news, they have not gotten past us!"

She then helped plan the ambush. The Muslims moved swiftly, and the element of surprise gave them victory. She and Dirar were united once more. Thus ends this tale of devotion, but Khawlah lived to fight many other battles with the Romans. May Allah reward this fearless knight.

~~~

From the characteristics of the Companions was their intense striving to fulfill the rights of their brothers and sisters in Islam. They would accompany them for Allah's sake, and not for any personal reasons. They would demand full rights for their brothers and sisters, but would not demand their own rights.

BRINGING IT FORWARD TO TODAY

This beautiful female knight was not told she couldn't do the deeds she did for her brother. She was a fierce fighter, but had great religiosity and morals; learning to fight for what was right. We as women can be true warriors for Allah in many ways, one of the most important of which is learning all we can about our *deen* and passing it on, along with an enduring love for Allah, to our next generation. This is striving which will reap benefits for decades to come.

Did You Know?

It was said about this Muslim woman, Zubaidah bint Jaf'ar, that she was forgiven with the first shovelful of dirt.

This wealthy and intelligent woman from the 9th century changed a desolate and deserted route to one teeming with life.

She constructed a series of waterways from Baghdad to Makkah, and used engineers to design wells, reservoirs, and pools for the pilgrims going over 900 miles to Hajj, most of it rocky terrain!

This venture cost her many millions of Dinars, and along the waterway she built cafes, workshops, and mosques.

You can still see remnants of this waterway in and around Makkah, and this was appropriately called Zubaidah's way.

This route helped transform these highways around Baghdad into the trading center of the Muslim world, and people used to say that this period was one long wedding day and an everlasting feast.

This eloquent lover of the Qur'an was a pioneer in the field of construction.

It is said that her palace sounded like a beehive because of the sounds of the one hundred women she employed who unceasingly recited the Qur'an day and night.

The Bounty of Asceticism

"And whoever fears Allah, He will make for him a way out, and will provide for him from where he does not expect. And whoever relies upon Allah, then He is sufficient for him. Indeed, Allah will accomplish His purpose." {The Qur'an, 65:3}

Is wealth ours to grasp, or should we allow it to run through our fingers like sand scooped up in a desert. Is it ours to hoard, or should we trust in the provisions ordained for us that gently descend like steady rain. Look to the birds as they go out each day, gathering, and come back to their nest sated. Are we not more beloved to our Creator than these bastions of aerial freedom?

Imagine a stark room with no worldly touch in it, imagine the basest of foods to exist on, imagine no distractions to your worship and trek to the Hereafter. This was the earthly life of a companion very close to our Prophet (pbuh).

Abu Dharr Al-Ghifari

Quote: *"Declare your jihad on thirteen enemies you cannot see – egoism, arrogance, conceit, selfishness, greed, lust, intolerance, anger, lying, cheating, gossiping and slandering. If you can master and destroy them, then you will be ready to fight the enemy you can see."*
–Al Ghazali

Abu Dharr Al-Ghifari was from the tribe of Ghifar, and they lived on money given to them by caravans to and from Syria. Sometimes, regrettably, this money was not always given willingly. Abu Dharr stood out from his tribe with his boldness, seriousness of mind, and foresight. He was disturbed by the idols being worshipped, and he disavowed the corruptness and shallow superstitions around him. When he heard of the new prophet in Makkah, he was immediately interested, and he sent his brother to see about him. When his brother returned, Abu Dharr didn't get the answers he was looking for. His burning heart needed that which would bring it coolness and truth, so he asked his brother, "Can you provide for my family while I go to see this man for myself?"

"Yes," his brother answered, "But, beware of the people of Makkah. They are against all those who follow him"

Abu Dharr set out the next morning with some anxiety about the persecution he had heard was going on in Makkah, and decided he would be very careful who he asked. When he reached Makkah, he was weary and so he lay down to sleep in the masjid. Ali, the cousin of the Prophet (pbuh) walked by him, and graciously invited him to come and stay in his house. Having just met him, Abu Dharr was nervous to ask Ali about the Prophet (pbuh), and didn't find out anything about his quest the next day. On that second night, again, Ali invited him to his house. Islamically, you are not to ask a guest in your home any questions until the third day, so Ali waited until the third night, and finally asked Abu Dharr why he had come to Makkah. Abu Dharr felt comfortable to open up to his kindhearted host and responded, "I have come wishing to meet the new prophet, and to hear of what he says."

Ali's face lit up as he poured out his heart to his guest, and told him many wonderful things about the Prophet (pbuh). "Would you like to meet him?"

"Oh, yes!" Abu Dharr responded, and Ali told him to follow him to the Prophet's (pbuh) house in the morning, and "if there is no danger, we will enter his home."

The two quickly and quietly moved down the dusty streets until they were sure they weren't followed and entered the Prophet's home. There they found a man with a radiant face and calm demeanor. Abu Dharr smiled and said, "Peace be upon you, Oh, Messenger of Allah."

"Peace, mercy, and blessings of Allah be upon you too," answered the Prophet (pbuh). Abu Dharr's heart leapt in his chest and he immediately became Muslim, being one of only a handful to accept Islam at that time.

The Prophet (pbuh) spent many days teaching him about the way of Islam and how to read and understand the Qur'an, but Abu Dharr was told not to tell anyone in Makkah about becoming Muslim. Abu Dharr heard this warning, but his heart was bursting with the light and beauty of his new-found religion, and he firmly exclaimed, "I swear by the One Who holds my soul in His Hand, I cannot leave Makkah before going to the masjid and crying out to the Quraish with the call to truth!"

He looked for a reaction, but when the blessed Prophet didn't say anything, Abu Dharr set out and entered the Kaaba. He called out, loudly and boldly, the Declaration of Faith, raising the anger and wrath of the Quraish gathered around him. They started beating him so badly that the uncle of the Prophet (pbuh) had to shield him. He lay on the ground bruised and broken and when he regained consciousness, he went back to the Messenger (pbuh). The Prophet (pbuh) said, "Did I not tell you not to declare your conversion to Islam in public?"

"Oh, Messenger of Allah," Abu Dharr answered, "it was a necessary rite of passage for me. I would do it again for the peace it brings."

Abu Dharr felt ready then to go back to his tribe, and there he converted his brother, mother, and, with his new conviction, finally gained enough converts to establish daily prayers. Abu Dharr remained in his homeland through the battle of Badr. This, the first of the Muslims' battles, was fought because the Quraish had tortured and abused the Muslims, and when they migrated, took all that they owned in Makkah and put it on a caravan to Syria. The Muslims went out with a small force to get it back, but never saw the caravan. Instead, Allah sent them to fight to establish the truth in the land. He also missed the Battle of Uhud, fought because the Quraish wanted revenge for their loss at Badr, and he was absent for the Battle of the Trench, where, against what the enemy thought was an overwhelming force, the Muslims were victorious. When the time was right, Abu Dharr went to Madina to serve the Prophet (pbuh).

Abu Dharr remained in the company of this great and noble man, benefitting from all he was able to learn and observe.

After the Prophet's (pbuh) death, he was so crushed by the change in peoples' hearts that he moved to Syria. When Uthman became Khalifah, Abu Dharr saw even more of a path away from the truth so evident in the Prophet's (pbuh) life, and became very outspoken about it. He moved to Damascus, and was horrified to see the materialism there, publicly announcing his disapproval. He moved to Madina, and felt the same aversion, so Uthman mercifully ordered him to move to a small village outside of Madina where he spent the rest of his days, far from other people and uncaring about material wealth, preferring the simple spiritual life of one who was waiting to leave at any moment.

A man once visited him and asked, "Where are your possessions?"

Abu Dharr answered, "We have a home elsewhere, and we send all our good things there."

The man said, "But, do you not need things as long as you are living in this home?"

Abu Dharr's answer was simple.

"The landlord is not going to allow us to stay here." This is how he lived and died in truth and without adornment, pleased with his Lord as his provision.

~~~

From the characteristics of the Companions (ra), was the feeling that the world was not precious. They felt it was insignificant. As the Prophet (pbuh) said, "If the world meant as much as a wing of a mosquito to Allah, he would not have let the disbeliever take a sip of water from it."

Maalik bin Deenar said that the world was uglier than magic, as it separates a slave from his Master.

One of the Companions said, "If you want to be close to Allah, then put an iron wall between yourself and your desires."

Bringing it Forward to Today

We all have "things". We love our "things". We use them every day. But do we use them for good or for distraction. They are going

Unearthing Hidden Jewels

to be left behind when we die, (and that could be at any time!), and eventually every "thing" will turn to dust. Do we remember when we reach for our "things" that we will face our Lord one day, and He will ask us how we used these "things". Let us bring good to all that we "own" so we can go to Him with a tranquil heart. One scholar said, "Oh, Caliph, for you to keep company with a person who makes you afraid of the Hereafter is better than one who gives you safety here."

Did You Know?

Abu al-Qasim Khalaf Ibn Abbas al-Zahrawi (930-1013 CE) known to the west as Abulcasis, was the most eminent surgeon among Muslim physicians of his time and beyond. In his famous book, *Al-Tas'rif,* he described and illustrated more than two hundred surgical instruments, many of which he, himself, devised. He stressed the importance of the study of Anatomy as a fundamental prerequisite to surgery and his description of varicose vein stripping, even after ten centuries, is close to modern surgical techniques. Zahrawi described hemophilia for the first time in medical history. He advocated the reimplantation of a fallen tooth, and the use of a dental prosthesis carved from cow's bone. He appears to be the first surgeon in history to use cotton (an Arabic word) in surgical dressings in the control of hemorrhage, as padding in the splinting of fractures, and as a vaginal padding in fractures of the pubic bone. He introduced a method for the removal of kidney stones by cutting into the urinary bladder. He was the first to teach the lithotomic position with legs in stirrups for vaginal operations and he described the tracheotomy procedure in great detail.

Surgeons all over the world today unknowingly practice procedures that Muslim surgeons introduced over 1,000 years ago.

The Jewel of Asceticism

"Beautified for people is the love of that which they desire – of women and sons, heaped-up sums of gold and silver, fine branded horses, and cattle and tilled land. That is the enjoyment of worldly life, but Allah has with Him the best return."
{The Qur'an, 3:14}

Salmon, an empty bucket, and the infinity sign …, what do these three seemingly diverse objects have to do with the flow of wealth? The shimmering, multi-hued salmon valiantly fight their way upstream, struggling to the place of their birth, only to lay their eggs and then succumb, giving their very life so that these eggs can grow to their full strength and swim the same circuit, creating a never-ending cycle of life and death. So too, when we give a small "egg" of charity in the sake of Allah, it grows by His Grace, to a creature of movement, swimming through the earth bringing good, only to be returned to us in a way that we might give again, keeping the cycle of giving alive. Oh, yes…the empty bucket. If you leave an empty bucket under a faucet with a single drip, will it not, in time, eventually fill, and even overflow? This is the hope we have in the charity we give, that our "bucket" will overflow onto the scale of good deeds on that Inevitable Day.

Let us read about a master of this flow…

Sa'id bin 'Amir Al-Jamahi

Quote: *"Repentance and yearning, and yearning and repentance: this is the total harvest of life."* –Khurram Murad, *'Dying And Living For Allah'*

Asceticism

Sa'id bin "Amir Al-Jumahi was among thousands who answered the call of the chieftains of the tribe of Quraish to come and witness the death of Khubayb bin Adiy, a companion of the Prophet (pbuh). The tribe believed they would take revenge for the battle of Badr by killing this loyal man of God, and through the shouts of the women and children surrounding the prisoner, Sa'id heard the captive's calm, steady voice saying, "If you would allow me to make two rak'ahs of prayer before my death, then do so."

Sa'id watched as Khubayb took his stance in the direction of the Kabbah, and after he prayed two beautiful, dignified rak'ahs, Sa'id saw him turn to the leaders of Quraish saying, "I swear by Allah that if I didn't believe you would think I was taking too long out of fear of death, I would have prayed much more."

The crowd then starting beating and dismembering him as they asked him, "Would you like Muhammad to be in your place, and for you to be safe in his place?"

As the life bled out of Khubayb, he replied, "By Allah, I would not wish to be safe and secure with my wife and children if Muhammad were to be pricked by a thorn because of it!"

The frenzied crowd then screamed, "Kill him! Kill him!"

Sa'id then saw Khubayb's vision turn to the heavens as he said, "Our God, count their numbers and exterminate them! Leave not one of them alive!"

This tranquil spirit was then lifted, surrendering to its Creator's decree.

Sa'id was not able to get this scene out of his head, dreaming of the serenity of this man on the very spot he was being killed. The curse he made rang in the young man's ears, and he feared for his life.

Khubayb, in his death, taught Sa'id that true life is one of belief, and fighting for the sake of that belief with strength of faith and honor. Anyone who could inspire such feelings in a man must surely be a prophet sent from heaven. Sometimes death begets life, and Sa'id's heart was opened to Islam. He proclaimed his new faith publicly, renouncing the tribe of Quraish and their evil deeds and idols.

He traveled to Madina in search of his heart's desire, and became a constant companion to the Blessed Prophet (pbuh). When the Prophet (pbuh) died, Sa'id became a sword in the hands of Abu Bakr (ra), and Umar (ra), performing many heroic deeds in the battle of Yarmook.

One time, Sa'id had heard that Abu Bakr (ra) was planning to put him at the head of the Muslim army headed for Shaam, but as he waited patiently for the appointment, he heard that Abu Bakr, instead, had put Yazid ibn Abu Sufyan in charge and the army had already left. He immediately went to Abu Bakr (ra) and humbly asked if he could go and fight with Yazid. After much poetic truth and supplication for one another, Abu Bakr said, "Enough, Sa'id. I will send you there as head of the troops who will back Yazid in battle." When Sa'id arrived on the battle front, there was never a question about who was in charge. Sa'id bravely fought under the capable leadership of Yazid.

Umar (ra) was so pleased with Sa'id that he chose him to be the governor of Hims, and Sa'id begged him not to tempt him with worldly vanities. Umar stood fast, proclaiming, "You have put me as caliphate, and now you want to desert me?"

Sa'id knew Umar was resolute, so he relented. Umar asked him what salary he would need to do this job.

Sa'id replied, "What would I do with this salary, oh Commander of the Faithful? It would exceed my needs."

With Sa'id as governor, travelers to the Khalifa from Hims gave Umar a list of the poor in their city. Sa'id's name was there on the list, and this made Umar weep. He ordered a thousand dinars to be sent to Hims for Sa'id's expenses, with an appeal that he please use it.

When Sa'id saw this money, he exclaimed, "Surely, we belong to Allah, and to Him shall we return," as if a disaster had befallen him. His wife ran to him and asked if Umar had died, or more Muslims had died in battle, and he said to her that a bigger calamity than that had happened.

"The vanity of this world has come to me to ruin my chance of a share in the Hereafter, and temptation has entered my home!"

His prudent wife advised him to rid himself of this burden, and he asked her to help, so they hurriedly divided the money into many small bags and distributed it to the poor and destitute.

As time went on, many complaints began to filter in to Umar from the citizens of Hims regarding their governor, so Umar summoned Sa'id to him. Umar read him the list of complaints, and Sa'id addressed them one by one:

"He does not come and attend to our affairs until late in the morning."

Unearthing Hidden Jewels

Sa'id was reluctant to disclose his reason, but finally said that his wife had no servant, so he would get up early and knead dough, wait for it to rise, and then bake bread for his family. Then he would make ablution and go out to the people.

"He is never available to be seen at night."

Again, with reluctance, he told him that the daytime was for the people, and the night was spent in worship of Allah.

"One day every month, he does not come out at all!"

To this he said that he had no servant, and no clothing but what was on his back, and once a month he would wash them and that it took a whole day for them to dry so he could go out again.

"He faints from time to time and loses consciousness."

Sa'id quietly said that after what he witnessed with Khubayb, and the fact that he did not come forth to aid him, he feared that Allah would not forgive him, and then he would become overcome and faint.

Umar said at this point, "Praise be to Allah Who has not disappointed me in you."

Again he sent a thousand dinars to Sa'id's home, and when Sa'id and his wife saw this, he said to her, "We will give this to the One Who can return it for us when we will need it most!" and, on the spot, they divided the money into portions and gave it to the widows, orphans, and the poor.

Sa'id died at the young age of forty, pushing the life away until the very last moment, preferring to be pleasing to Allah, and wanting His

Asceticism

Lord's reward more than anything in this world. May he be surrounded with luxuriant abundance for all time.

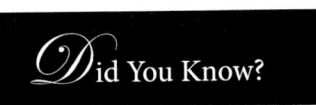

~~~

From the characteristics of the Companions (ra) was their attaching priority to working for the Hereafter. They would give priority to their portion of remembrance of Allah after the *Fajr* prayer over any other thing and priority to the night prayer over sleeping under a warm blanket.

The Messenger of Allah said, "Whoever's worries are of the Afterlife, Allah puts richness in his heart. He corrects his affairs and the world will be compelled to come to him. But, whoever's greatest worries are of the world, Allah puts poverty in front of his eyes. His affairs are put in disarray, and no worldly gain will come to him, except what has already been written for him."

BRINGING IT FORWARD TO TODAY

How do we define wealth? Is it what we own, or the complete contentment with what we have. Is it our things, or those things just outside the touch of our fingertips when we open our hands skyward in supplication. Remember the solitude of the grave, and desire will recede like the breakers of the ocean. Remember the gifts waiting with Allah, and your heart will swell with a yearning so deep, all else will fade.

Did You Know?

Al Kindi, a Muslim from the 9th century, was called one

of the twelve giant minds of history. He laid down the foundation of modern-day optics. His painstaking work led Ibn al-Haitham, the 10th-century Muslim mathematician, astronomer and physicist to the theory of light rays. Ibn Haitham was the first person to realize that light enters the eye, rather than leaving it. The ancient Greeks thought our eyes emitted rays, like a laser, which enabled us to see, but Ibn Haitham disproved this. He also invented the first pin-hole camera after noticing the way light came through a hole in his window shutters. This light projected an image on his wall of the outside. He worked out from this observation that the smaller the hole, the better the image, and was able then to set up the first Camera Obscura (from the Arab word *qamara* for a dark or private room), which was the first pinhole camera. He confirmed that light travels in a straight line and, he also was able to explain why the images were upside down (light come in on an angle and reflects up). The image coming through this pinhole could be traced onto a drawing surface, producing a picture.

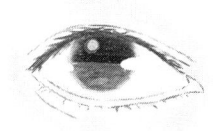

This brilliant man also made contributions to physics, astronomy, mathematics, ophthalmology, philosophy, and visual perception, studying about light and how it moves, and goes into the human eye. He wrote a book called the *Book of Optics*, which was translated into Latin by a medieval scholar, one section clearly showing how to see a spectrum of light.

We have much in the modern world to be thankful to him for.

The Futility of Wealth

"O Prophet, sufficient for you is Allah and for whoever follows you of the believers." {The Qur'an, 8:64}

Caterpillars are earthbound creatures, slowly gathering bits of food as they ripple along a leaf, accumulating their daily provision from their Creator. When they become heavy and sated with His bounty, they spin a cocoon around themselves, holding tight to the mass they have gathered, cloaking themselves to complete their cathartic metamorphosis. In a miracle known only to Allah, they transform into an elegant creature who sheds all that the caterpillar has accumulated and spreads its silky, resplendent wings to take flight. Daintily it flutters from one flower to the next, grateful to be free from the stifling existence of the temporal world.

Similarly, how, then, can man rise up to his potential if he is burdened by that which he amasses.

This companion left his possessions for Allah's sake, as one would leave something of no worth on the side of the road…

Suhaib Rumi

Quote: *"The lifetime distracts and preoccupies the heart and body, but asceticism, not giving importance to worldly things, gives rest to the heart and body. Verily, Allâh will ask us about the good things we enjoyed, so what about the forbidden!"* – Al Hasan Al Basri

The Holy Prophet (pbuh) said of him, "Suhaib is the first fruit of Rum (Turkey)."

Unearthing Hidden Jewels

Born in Iraq, his father was appointed governor of Ubullah. One day, the Romans ruthlessly attacked his father's city and took Suhaib (ra) prisoner as a child. The father could find no trace of him, so, after a very long search, gave up hope of ever seeing his son again. Suhaib was brought up among the Romans, and when he grew to be a strong young man, was sold as a slave to a man in Makkah. His master in Makkah, a very kind man, saw such wonderful qualities in Suhaib that he taught him the skills of trade, and then offered to set him free. Suhaib gratefully accepted his freedom, and although an outsider, started a business and became quite wealthy. He was very social, with a good sense of humor. He had a lovely acquaintance with the Prophet (pbuh), and Suhaib took on many a good habit from him. When revelation came, Suhaib embraced Islam immediately, but because of lack of tribal ties, bore the brunt of that decision. He was teased and tortured mercilessly by the Quraish. Nothing shook his faith though, and when ordered to migrate to Madina, he gathered his belongings and got ready to leave. When the Quraish got word of this, they had other ideas. They followed him and said, "You came here penniless, and earned all of this wealth in Makkah. We will not let you leave and take it with you!"

Suhaib, pointed to his bow and said, "You know that I am one of the most skillful archers of Makkah. I will fight with this bow and my sword to the death if you come near me. The Quraish persisted, so finally Suhaib said, "If all you desire is my wealth, then if I leave it with you, will you let me go?"

The Quraish agreed to this, and Suhaib turned his back on his caravan of wealth and left for Madina. When he finally reached the blessed city, he was thrilled, but totally exhausted, extremely hungry, and one of his eyes was badly swollen from the blowing sand. The Prophet (pbuh) and some companions were sitting around eating dates, and when Suhaib, in his wretched state, saw the dates he could not restrain himself and fell on the tray, trying to get the dates to his mouth as quickly as he could. Umar (ra) said, "Oh Prophet of Allah (pbuh), look at the state of Suhaib! His eye is sore, yet he is eating dates!" Suhaib immediately answered back, "Yes, but I am eating from the other eye, which is alright." This prompt reply amused the Prophet (pbuh). After Suhaib had his fill, he sat back and told them the whole story, and the Prophet said, "You struck a profitable bargain."

Suhaib always came forward and put his life on the line in the most challenging battles, using his skill in archery to fight in the way of Allah. Suhaib said, "I never allowed the Prophet (pbuh) to be between me and the enemy until he (pbuh) passed away." Suhaib's arrow hit the mark in all aspects of his life, as he helped the poor, gave in charity, and lavishly entertained his guests. People used to say that he was so generous that it bordered on extravagant, but he would answer them with a saying of the Prophet (pbuh), "Of you, the best is he who feeds the poor, and returns salutations."

He was so well respected that Umar (ra) on his deathbed instructed that Suhaib should lead his funeral prayers, and officiate as Iman until formal elections could be arranged.

How insignificant were the worldly possessions given up, but how immense the Divine blessings received!

~~~

From the characteristics of the Companions (ra) was that they didn't care about building nice houses. They would build only that which would meet their needs and nothing more. They didn't extend their hopes and desires for this world. One of the companions passed by someone building a house, so he recited this poem:

Do you build houses for the immortal?
If you thought, you would see your staying there is little
Under the shade of a stick is enough for him,
Whom one day departure will embrace him

BRINGING IT FORWARD TO TODAY

Our bargain with Allah as Believers is that we strive with our wealth and our persons in His Way, and He gives us nothing less than Paradise! Could we give up our possessions right now, everything we own? If it meant moving to the next level of righteousness, could we distribute our wealth until we were down to the bare essentials, keeping only enough so as not to beg? Allah doesn't ask us for that, but we should, at least, visualize this freeing scenario in our minds, and see what it feels like to have nothing but the clothes on our backs and our relationship with our Lord. This is a mirror with which to check the reflection we are putting out to the world. Let us redefine "desire", bringing it to a higher plain. Someone said, "Know that there is no poverty after Paradise, and no richness after the Hellfire."

Asceticism

Did You Know?

Many common words used in English today come from Arabic roots. Here are a few examples:

average, zero, jar, orange, hazard, lemon, lime, candy, magazine, mattress, chemistry, lilac, tarragon, tuna, guitar, gauze, cotton, cat, sofa, spinach, sorbet, safari.

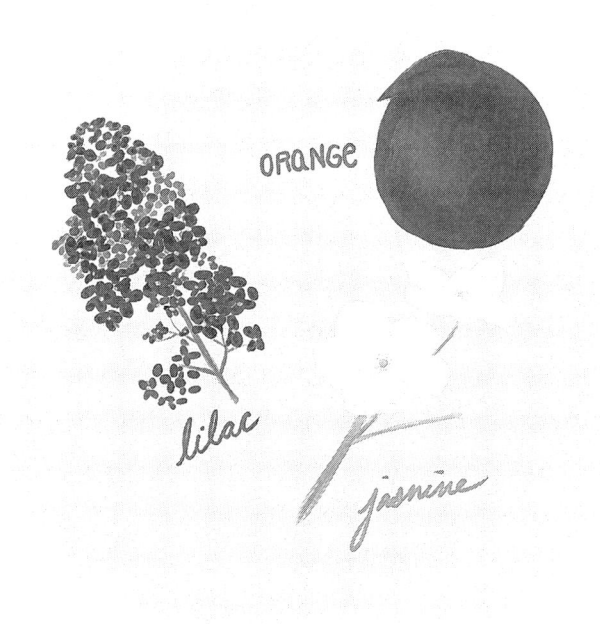

orange

lilac

jasmine

THE OFFERINGS OF A HEART IN FLOWER

"O you who have believed, shall I guide you to a bargain that will save you from a painful punishment? [It is that] you believe in Allah and His Messenger and strive your utmost in the cause of Allah with your wealth and your lives. That is best for you, if you but knew." {The Qur'an, 61:10-11}

Oh, wonder of wonders, that a tiny impassioned seed could bring such a plentiful yield of enlightenment. This sprout immediately opened her arms to the light and knowledge pouring forth upon her, reaching for it, knowing it was her means to grow. Soon, a bud of comprehension sprouted from her, and another, until she was a blossoming green tendril, wanting to take in all that she could from the goodness and truth around her. When a flower emerged, it was one of gentleness and sharing, and as she matured, the many priceless blossoms of insight combined to bring hope to the world. When her leaves had passed their time, the seeds of knowledge she had nurtured began to spread, encompassing a thriving generation of "seekers" like herself.

AISHA BINT ABU BAKR

Quote: *"Asceticism is not that you should not own anything, but that nothing should own you."* – Ali ibn Abu Talib

"Learn a portion of your religion from this red-hued lady." Aisha was the youngest wife of our Prophet (pbuh) and related over 2,210 stories of him so that his followers might know him for centuries to come. She was brought up by her father, who was well respected and

Asceticism

the closest friend of the noble Prophet, who had been a frequent visitor to their home since the very early days of his mission. In her youth, already known for her striking beauty and formidable memory, she came under the loving care and attention of the Prophet himself. Aisha became the Prophet's (pbuh) wife in Makkah when she was most likely in the tenth year of her life, but her wedding didn't take place until the second year after the Hijrah when she was about fourteen or fifteen years old.

She did not seem at all overawed by the thought of being wedded to the Messenger of God. About her wedding, she related that, shortly before she was to leave her parent's house, "I was playing on a see-saw and they came and took me from my play." They dressed her in a wedding-dress made from fine red-striped cloth from Bahrain, and in the presence of the smiling Prophet (pbuh), a bowl of milk was brought. There was no wedding feast, but it was clear that it was Aisha that he loved most.

As years wore on, she bore, along with the rest of the Prophet's household, poverty and hunger, and for days on end no fire would be lit in the sparsely furnished house for cooking or baking bread; they lived only on dates and water. Poverty did not cause her distress and self-sufficiency did not corrupt her lifestyle. During the last few years of the Prophet's (pbuh) life, he would make arrangements for his wives yearly expenses, but they gave most of it away in charity, and stayed content with the lives they had chosen. During the prophet's (pbuh) final illness, at the suggestion of his wives, it was to Aisha's apartment that he went. Aisha preserved for us these dying moments of the most honored of God's creation, His beloved Messenger, may He shower blessings on him, and she quoted him as saying at the time of death "O Lord, the Highest Companion," and these were the last words she heard him speak.

Aisha (ra) stuck to her choice of asceticism even after the Prophet (pbuh) died. When the Muslims were favored with enormous riches, she was given a gift of one hundred thousand dirhams. She was fasting when she received the money and distributed the entire amount to the poor, leaving not a thing for herself. Shortly afterwards, her maidservant said, "Could you buy meat for a dirham with which to break your fast?" and Aisha replied, "If I had remembered, I would have done so."

One day Abdullah, the son of Zubair, told those around him, "I have never met anyone more generous than my mother and my aunt." He was describing Asma and Aisha. He noted that their method of generosity was different. Aisha (ra) used to gather together, and then give out, while Asma (ra) would not keep anything in her hands for the next day. Both methods were the height of virtue.

Aisha was called *Umm al-Teeb* (the mother of fragrance), and was called that because she used to spray perfume on the money she donated. When asked why she did this, she explained that charity reaches Allah before the receiving person's hand so she wanted it to smell nice. She did this so often that it became her trademark and earned her this noble nickname.

Once, she was fasting on the day of Arafaat. It was extremely hot, and water was being sprinkled on her head. Aisha's (ra) brother told her to break her fast, as it was not necessary to keep a voluntary fast.

Asceticism

She said that since she had heard the Prophet (pbuh) say that the fast on the day of Arafat earns one the expiation of one year of sins, she would not give that up.

Whenever she spoke, she took over the junctures of hearts. She was a brilliant lamp of knowledge. A famous Imam remarked, "never did I see anyone more knowledgeable of the Qur'an, the laws of inheritance, the allowed and the forbidden, poetry, the history of the Arabs, Medicine, and Genealogy than this young woman." She never heard of a thing, but that she researched it carefully until she mastered it.

The life of Aisha (ra) was proof that a woman could be as learned as a man, and that she could be a teacher for many male scholars and experts. Her life was also proof that the same woman could be totally feminine, and a source of pleasure, joy, and comfort to her husband. Balance defines the life of a Muslim.

~~~

From the characteristics of the Companions is that they were not proud of their deeds, but would only see the deficiency of them. They would constantly, throughout their lives, be trying to perfect what was brought down to them, and would say, "Oh Allah, make me better than what they say, and forgive me for what they do not know."

Mutarrif ibn 'Abdullah (ra) said, "It is more beloved to me to spend the night sleeping and wake up regretful, than to spend the night standing in prayer and wake up proud of myself."

BRINGING IT FORWARD TO TODAY

Since when should we let youth get in the way of achieving great

Unearthing Hidden Jewels

things? We don't know what Allah has written for us at any age, and if our own distractions or lack of self-esteem stop us from realizing this goal from our Lord, then we are only half of what we could be. Just try...try to get involved in the community – you don't know where it may lead. Just try...try to design, build, seek knowledge, teach, join, purify, and master. Allah moves us forward in ways we could never imagine!

Did You Know?

Ibn Battuta, a Muslim Moroccan scholar and traveler, started on his journey in 1325 when he was 20 years old. His reason for travel was to realize the vivid dreams he was experiencing and to go on Pilgrimage to Makkah. Here is the start of his journey in his own words:

"My departure from Tangier, my birthplace, took place ... with the object of making the Pilgrimage to the Holy House [at Makkah] and of visiting the tomb of the Prophet [in Madina], God's richest blessing and peace be on him. I set out alone having neither fellow-traveler in whose companionship I might find cheer, nor caravan whose party I might join, but swayed by an overmastering impulse within me and a desire long-cherished in my bosom to visit these illustrious sanctuaries. So I braced my resolution to quit all my dear ones, female and male, and forsook my home as birds forsake their nests. My parents being yet in the bonds of life, it weighed sorely upon me to part from

Asceticism

them, and both they and I were afflicted with sorrow at this separation."

His traveling went on for 30 years, covering 75,000 miles. He visited over 40 countries, which were then under the leadership of the Muslims. He met many dangers, and had many adventures along the way. He was attacked by bandits, almost drowned in a sinking ship, and was nearly beheaded by a tyrant ruler.

His journeys included trips to North Africa, the Horn of Africa, West Africa, Eastern Europe, the Middle East, South Asia, Central Asia, Southeast Asia and China, a distance surpassing threefold of his contemporary Marco Polo. Ibn Battuta lived by the motto, "Never, if possible, cover any road a second time."

LOYALTY – THE UNWAVERING PROMISE

"And hold firmly to the rope of Allah all together and do not become divided. And remember the favor of Allah upon you – when you were enemies and He brought your hearts together and you became, by His favor, brothers. And you were on the edge of a pit of the Fire, and He saved you from it. Thus does Allah make clear to you His verses that you may be guided."
{The Qur'an, 3:103}

Soil, rich and deep brown, is loyal to the seedling, enclosing and protecting it as it matures; rain, cleansing and beneficial, is loyal to the soil, keeping it moist and flexible, helping it give way to the ripened fruit of the earth; sunlight, warming and nurturing, bringing forth its radiance and heat for the chemical reactions necessary for existence to flourish, is loyal to all three – they work together to bring us nourishment, beauty, shade, oxygen, variety, and a cooling of the eyes. They are bonded and symbiotic – a flowing covenant, one into the other forming an unbroken chain of rebirth, regeneration, and renewal. So, too, is this covenant of the brotherhood and sisterhood of Islam, blending the best of all peoples into an unbroken chain of revitalization for the soul of mankind.

It was a great day for Muslims when this companion swore his allegiance…

THUMAMAH BIN UTHAL

Quote: *"The human soul is a spiritual substance which is not a body possessing form, nor a substance restricted and limited."* – Abu Hamid Al-Ghazali, *'Mysteries of the Human Soul'*

Loyalty

In the 6th year of Hijrah, eight letters were sent by the Prophet (pbuh) to the Kings of Arabia and neighboring lands, calling them to Islam. One of these letters was received, with much contempt, by Thumamah bin Uthal. He arrogantly refused to listen, and began plotting to kill the Prophet (pbuh). He spent hours waiting to catch his prey alone, but the one time that this happened Thumamah's own uncle intervened, and his plan was thwarted. Frustrated, he decided to vent his anger on the followers of the Prophet (pbuh), and brutally slaughtered many of them, causing an edict that anyone who could dispatch this unruly King would be free of guilt in the eyes of Allah.

Not long after this, Thumamah decided to make the journey to the Kaaba to make sacrifices to his idols in the sanctuary. Unknown to him, the Prophet (pbuh) had set up patrols outside the city of Madina, and one such patrol caught Thumamah. Not knowing his identity, they took him to the masjid in Madina and tied him to one of the pillars. When prayer time came, the Prophet (pbuh) asked the men if they were aware of who they had captured.

"No, Messenger of Allah," they answered.

"This is Thumamah bin Uthal al-Hanafi, so treat him well," he told them.

The Prophet (pbuh) went home after the prayer and sent what food he had to Thumamah, along with fresh camel milk each morning and evening.

Finally, the Prophet (pbuh) went to him, hoping to get his allegiance to Islam, and said, "What have you to say for yourself, Thumamah?"

51

"If you kill me, it will be what I deserve for killing your people," he responded, "but if you grant me my life, you will have my gratitude. If you wish me to pay a ransom for myself, I will give you what you ask."

The Prophet (pbuh) simply turned and walked away, and this scene happened two more times over the next several days, with the question and response staying the same. Thumamah was fed and treated graciously this whole time, much to his confusion. After the third exchange, with the same results, the Prophet (pbuh) ordered him to be released. The companions were perplexed, but did as they were told. Thumamah left the masjid, mounted his camel and rode to a palm grove near the edge of Madina, and made full ablution in the spring there.

He doubled back to the masjid, and in front of the Muslims announced, "I bear witness that there is no god but Allah, and that Muhammad is the Messenger of Allah." He then said to the Prophet (pbuh), "I swear by Allah, that there was none on earth whose face I hated to see more than yours, Muhammad. Now, there is none whom I love to see more than you. Before this, there was not a religion which I despised more than yours, and now it is the most beloved of all religions to me. I even hated your town more than any place in the world, and now it is the place of which I am most fond."

He then asked what penance he should do for all the blood spilled of the companions, and the Prophet (pbuh) informed him that all of his previous sins were forgiven when he entered Islam.

Thumamah then uttered, "My sword and my person are at your disposal."

He then reminded the Prophet (pbuh) that he was on the way to make a visit to the Kaaba, and wondered if he should complete the ritual now that he was no longer pagan.

The Prophet (pbuh) said, "Go and perform the 'umrah, but do it for Allah alone, and in the way which He revealed it to me."

Thus, Thumamah was the first Muslim in history to perform the 'umrah as it is performed today. When the Quraish heard him declaring his faith, they rushed at him with anger, and a young man put arrow to bow and aimed it at him. Several men held the young man back saying, "Do not hasten our destruction! Do you not know who this is? It is Thumamah bin Uthal, king of al-Yamamah. If he is harmed his people will blockade our town and we will die of starvation!"

Thumamah declared to them, "I swear by the One Who is Lord of this House that after I return to al-Yamamah, you will not receive even a grain of wheat until every last one of you become Muslim."

Bit by bit the blockade took its toll, until the people of Makkah found themselves in dire straits. Nothing was available in the markets, and they truly feared that they and their children would starve to death. They wrote to the Prophet telling him of this, and he asked Thumamah to end the blockade and Thumamah, at once, complied.

Thumamah remained loyal to the Prophet (pbuh) and Islam, and after the death of the Prophet (pbuh) he warned the false prophet, Musaylamah, to desist from his dark deeds. When Musaylamah refused, Thumamah made war against the renegades, in the company of those who were also loyal to the faith, until there was victory for the righteous, helping to preserve the way of Allah for time immemorial.

Unearthing Hidden Jewels

~~~

From the characteristics of the companions (ra) was their desire to be in the company of the righteous, their ardent striving for the pure *Shari'ah*, and their feelings of disgrace for anyone who went towards the forbidden. They would never do a deed unless they knew that the pleasure of Allah was there, and they only hated and loved for Allah's sake, not for anything worldly.

The Prophet (pbuh) said:" Whoever possesses three things will find the sweetness of iman, for Allah and His Messenger to be more beloved to him than anything else, to love a person for Allah's sake alone, and to hate to return to disbelief the way he hates to be thrown into the fire."

Ahmad ibn Harb (ra) said, "There is nothing more beneficial to a Muslim's heart than to mix with the righteous and to watch their actions, while nothing is more harmful to the heart than mixing with the sinners and watching their actions."

Bringing it Forward to Today

Allah gave us the key to loyalty with our brothers and sisters, and that key is "*Assalamulaikum*" or "Peace be with you", the Islamic greeting of all the prophets throughout time. Adam greeted the angels with this, and these words do more to bond heart to heart than any other words spoken. This soothing declaration can melt even the harshest of words, and heal the deepest of wounds perpetrated on a soul. Give *salams* warmly and often. It is the tie that binds. Abu Qulamah Al-Jirmi in a sermon once said, "If you hear something you don't like about your brother, try your best to seek an excuse for him. If you do not find an excuse, then say, "Maybe he has an excuse I don't know about."

Did You Know?

Right in the center of Tibet, known for being the core of Buddhism, there is a masjid which was the product of many deeply ingrained cultural contacts between the Islamic world, Central Asia, and the Himalayas. These contacts began before the eighth century and continue through this present day. In the 12th century a group of Muslim traders from Kashmir and Ladakh arrived in Tibet as merchants. They settled there and married Tibetan women, who then converted to Islam. It is said that marriages and social situations increased the Tibetan Muslim population, and today there is a large and thriving community around the capital, Lhasa.

The story of the masjid there began with the 5th Dali Llama (1617-1682) when a teacher who was Muslim went everyday to a hill outside of the city to do his prayers. The Dali Llama watched him with interest for a few days, and then summoned him. The Muslim explained to him that he was worshipping according to the tenets of his religion, and the leader was so impressed that he sent an archer to the hill, and arrows were shot in all four directions, with the land within the arrows being deeded to the Muslim community. On that land was built the first masjid and cemetery for the Muslims, and it is still there today. The Muslims were also allowed to govern by Islamic law, and had their own shops , with no taxes levied on them.

Unearthing Hidden Jewels

True of Heart, Noble of Deed

"And Allah put affection in their hearts. If you had spent all that is in the earth, you could not have brought their hearts together; but Allah brought them together. Indeed, He is Exalted in Might, Wise." {The Qur'an, 8: 63}

Once an evil, vile, jealous creature of the earth decided he would try and destroy a magnificent mountain where goodness made its home. He first tried sending the unrelenting assault of a hurricane, but the lashing torrent only served to mold the mountain by the flowing wisdom of the cascading water. He then tried a tornado hoping to shake this towering rock to its very roots, but it only pared away the mountain's rough edges, making it more beautiful. His last attempt was the chaotic onslaught of blinding thunderbolts, but this only spread the mountain's goodness throughout the land.

What evil can destroy a mountain as it reaches for the sky and closeness to its Lord? It is under the wing of the most gentle of Protectors.

This Companion was described as having the clearest face, the best manners, and the most solid sense of decency.

Abu 'Ubaydah bin Al-Jarrah

Quote: "Piety is the connection to the past. " – Sheikh Safi Khan

Abu 'Ubaydah, one of the ten promised Paradise before they left this earth, was a very early convert to Islam. He declared his faith one day after Abu Bakr (ra). He was taken by Abu Bakr (ra) directly to the Prophet (pbuh), and became part of the bedrock that Islam was built on at that time. He was tall, slim, and graceful, and all felt peace in his calming presence. This charismatic man had to endure the torment from the pagans of Makkah, something which helped make him stronger in his belief. He emigrated to Abyssinia, but came back to fight in *jihad*. He later emigrated to Madina, giving him the title of 'The Man who Emigrated Twice'.

His loyalty through it all was to Allah and His Messenger, so much so that the Prophet (pbuh) said of him, "Every *ummah* has one who is to be trusted, and the trustworthy one for this *ummah* is Abu 'Ubaydah." He was there at the battle of Badr, charging through the enemy, trying to end this threat wherever and however he could. One man was very persistent in his pursuit of Abu 'Ubaydah during the heat of the battle, and Abu 'Ubaydah tried to flee from him over and over again, but this man would not give up. Finally, Abu 'Ubaydah had no choice but to raise his sword and sever the head of his own pagan father. This severing was the embodiment of the sadness endured by the Muslims who stood by what they believed. Allah revealed a verse about Abu 'Ubaydah in the Quran, 58: 22: "*You will not find a people who believe in Allah and the Last Day having affection for those who oppose Allah and His Messenger, even if they were their fathers or their sons or their brothers or their kindred. He has decreed within their hearts faith and supported them with spirit from Him. And We will admit them to gardens beneath which rivers flow, wherein they abide eternally. Allah is pleased with them, and they are pleased with Him – those are the party of Allah. Unquestionably, the party of Allah – they are the successful.*"

Unearthing Hidden Jewels

One day a group from Yemen who had recently converted to Islam came to the Prophet (pbuh) asking him to send one of his honest and righteous Companions to teach them about their *deen*. The Prophet (pbuh) told them to return in the evening and he would have the right person for them. Umar said of that moment that he "never wished to be given command as much as on that day, for I wished to be considered strong and trustworthy." The Prophet (pbuh) was scanning the crowd after prayer that night, and Umar pulled himself up to his full height, but the Prophet (pbuh) chose Abu 'Ubaydah, much to Umar's resignation.

During the defeat of the battle of Uhud, the unbelievers were looking to kill the Prophet (pbuh), and Abu 'Ubaydah was one of the ten who surrounded him, protecting him to the death if that became necessary. After the battle had ended, one of the teeth of the Prophet (pbuh) had been broken, his head had a gash in it, and two of the rings from his vest of chain mail were driven deeply into his cheek. Abu 'Ubaydah swore he alone knew how to remove these rings without hurting the Prophet (pbuh), so he caught the rings in his teeth, losing his two incisors in the process. Abu Bakr commented, "He was indeed rare, for he was still handsome, even with his teeth missing."

When victory came to the Muslims, Abu 'Ubaydah was put at the head of those getting ready to enter Makkah, an honor given only to him.

After the death of the Prophet (pbuh), the Muslims were like a group of sheep on a rainy night. Dazed and confused, they needed leadership to bring them back together. The Companions gathered to choose their next Amir, and Abu Bakr grabbed Abu 'Ubaydah by the hand and asked him to be caliphate, but Abu 'Ubaydah wisely said that he could not go ahead of someone that the Prophet (pbuh) chose to lead the prayer." He was the first to pledge allegiance to Abu Bakr, and this move was crucial to the *ummah* at that point.

When fighting the Romans in Shaam, he was victorious over a great army and won the city of Homs, treating the people there so well that they became Muslim. The Roman leader was so angry he gathered a great army to come to fight there. Abu Ubaydah called for backup, and Abu Bakr sent Khalid ibn Waleed to lead in the defense of Homs. In the midst of the heat of battle, word came to Abu 'Ubaydah that Abu Bakr had died, and Umar, the new leader, wanted him to take over the leadership of the army there. He felt it was not right to do this at a critical time of the battle, and so waited until Khalid had a stunning victory, and then shared the message with him. Khalid said, "What stopped you from telling me about this?"

Humbly, Abu 'Ubaydah said, "We are not here to seek worldly power, nor do we fight for the sake of this life. We are brothers for the sake of Allah!"

After Umar assumed leadership, Abu 'Ubaydah led an army of Muslims in Syria. When a plague struck, which was claiming the lives of many Muslims, Umar summoned Abu 'Ubaydah with an urgent letter, but Abu 'Ubaydah said, "I know why the Commander of the Faithful is in need of me. He wishes to extend the life of one who is not destined to remain with him." He sent Umar a letter asking him to excuse him from obeying this order, and that he would stay and allow Allah to decide his fate. Umar wept when he received this letter, to the point that the Muslims around him asked if Abu 'Ubaydah had died. Umar replied, "No, but death is close to him."

The plague finally reached Abu 'Ubaydah, and on his deathbed he had words of admonition for those around him, saying, "Fear Allah, and abide by His orders. If any human were to live a thousand years, there is no doubt he will have the same end as that you see before you. The cleverest one is the one more obedient to Allah, and the one who has good deeds for the Hereafter." He then gave his *salams*, turned to Mu'adh ibn Jabal (ra) and asked him to lead the prayer, and breathed his last.

Mu'adh (ra) rose and said to the people, "You have lost a man, I swear by Allah, never have I seen the like in his generosity of spirit, freedom from spite and hatred, love for the Hereafter, and commitment to the well-being of the people."

Abu 'Ubaydah (ra) was loyal from his first breath as a Muslim to his last.

~~~

From the characteristics of the Companions was that they were constantly letting go of that which no longer served their religion, and tried to take on that which was pleasing to their Lord. Yahya ibn Muadh (ra), said of the believers they must be full of modesty, harmless, full of goodness, and not corrupt. Their tongues must be truthful, the words to be little, and they must be plentiful in good actions. They must not be excessive, and must be good to their relatives, be dignified and grateful, full of contentment, forbearing, friendly to their brothers, compassionate and chaste. They should not curse, insult, backbite, or gossip, and should not be hasty, envious, hateful, arrogant, or vain. They should not lean towards worldliness, and should not sleep too much. They should not be absent-minded, nor show-off, or be hypocritical, or selfish. They should be soft, cheerful, and loving for the sake of Allah. Their struggle should be for the afterlife.

BRINGING IT FORWARD TO TODAY

If we chose ten characteristics of a firm believer like Abu 'Ubaydah and worked on them one at a time, giving each one a month of our attention, in ten months would we not be significantly better? Goodness takes practice, just like memorizing the Qur'an or studying your math homework. Let's all vow to take this coming year to be first in our *deen*. Who knows, this could be the year that we meet our Lord, and would we then not meet him with a striving heart? Ahh… the delicious fragrance of Paradise…

Did You Know?

Al-Jazari was a 13th Century mechanical engineer and the father of modern robotics. Some of his inventions and designs included the combination lock, a musical automaton, which was a boat with four automatic musicians that floated on a lake, a "peacock fountain" which was a sophisticated hand washing device featuring humanoid automata as servants which offered soap and towels, and an early water supply system driven by gears and hydropower.

He wrote a book called, *A Compendium on the Theory and Practice of the Mechanical Arts*, which included fifty devices, grouped into six categories. His seven-meter high Elephant clock used Greek water-raising technology, an Indian elephant, an Egyptian phoenix, Arabian figures, a Persian carpet, and Chinese dragons, thereby celebrating the diversity of the world. It incorporated several mechanisms that are presently used in modern engineering, such as automata, flow regulators, and a closed-loop system. The clock was driven by gravitational force. Periodically, a metal ball dropped out of a magazine at the top of the device. Triggered by the metal ball, a bowl inside the elephant would slowly sink into a bucket as it filled with water. As this float descended, it powered the clock's mechanisms and time-signals. At the end of the cycle, the bowl emptied and returned to the top to repeat the process. The clock would keep running as long as there were metal balls in the magazine.

Ibn Battuta enthusiastically described this wondrous clock in his book of travels.

SAFEGUARDING THE DEEN

"The believing men and believing women are allies of one another. They enjoin what is right and forbid what is wrong and establish prayer and give zakah and obey Allah and His Messenger. Those - Allah will have mercy upon them. Indeed, Allah is Exalted in Might and Wise." {The Qur'an, 9:71}

How often do we think about the fascinating design of our bodies? When do we ponder the marvel of how the heart, the stopwatch of our lives, keeps beating from the time it forms in the womb until our last moments on this earth? It is hunkered down in the cradle of the ribs, and these watchful guardians use might and main to protect their benefactor. The stalwart skeleton is unfailing in its support of the supple tendons that allow growth and movement, while the resilient muscles bring robustness and vigor to our intended actions. The pliant skin is like a coat of armor, impenetrable, consistent, and dutiful in its role as a shield from harm to what is contained within its walls. The surging blood removes toxins and carries the light of oxygen needed to thrive, sustain, and replenish. All of these functional gifts toil to be the sheath for our internal soul.

So too, this champion of the believers took on the role of cloak of Islam, protecting and shielding the heart of the *ummah* from its enemies.

HAMZA IBN 'ABD AL-MUTTALIB

Quote: *"The Prophet (pbuh), peace and blessings be upon him, said: "My Companions are as stars. Whomsoever of them you follow, you will*

Unearthing Hidden Jewels

be rightly guided." When a man looks at a star, and finds his way by it, the star does not speak any word to that man. Yet, by merely looking at the star, the man knows the road from the unknown trail and reaches his goal." — Rumi

Hamza, the 'Lion of Islam', was the Prophet (pbuh)'s uncle and foster brother, and there was not much difference in their ages. The two grew up to be quite different, Muhammad (pbuh) quiet, and unassuming, and Hamza strong and brave, letting no man challenge him. He loved to roam the desert, and was excellent in the art of wrestling, swordsmanship, and archery. In the beginning, he did not pay much attention to Islam. He was deeply attached to his worldly pursuits, but Allah guided him in a way unlike any other.

One day he was returning from a hunt and a slave girl approached him and told him that his nephew had been preaching his religion in the Kaaba when Abu Jahl began abusing him. Hamza was told that Muhammad (pbuh) sadly went away, which raised his anger even more. He headed straight for the Kaaba and when he saw Abu Jahl, he jumped on him and hit him with his bow on the head, causing much damage. It was said to him by the Quraish that he must have forsaken his beliefs, and he replied, "If truth dawns on me, who is there to check me! Well, I declare here and now that Muhammad (pbuh) is The Prophet of Allah, and whatever he says is true. By Allah, I cannot go against Islam." When Abu Jahl saw Hamza so angry, he left him alone.

When Hamza went home, he began to realize the import and responsibility of what he had done. He had accepted Islam culturally,

Loyalty

in sympathy and defense of his cousin, but what did his heart have to say? He spent that night restless, and agonizing over not knowing the truth, so he prayed, "Oh, Allah, if this matter is right for me, then put faith in my heart. If not, then show me a way out of what I have vowed." In the morning, he went straight to The Prophet's (pbuh) house to ask for his help in sorting it all out. The Prophet (pbuh) patiently explained the wisdom of Islam, and then warned of the Fire and told of the beauty of the Paradise. Allah opened Hamza's heart to the truth, and he declared, "I would not wish to have everything the sun shines upon while I follow my previous religion. I know when I am out in the desert that God is not held in the Kaaba." This came in the 6th year of revelation.

With Hamza's acceptance of Islam, everything changed for the Muslims in Makkah. Now the enemies of Islam had to think twice before causing harm to one of the believers, and Hamza proclaimed his religion openly, which was not done before. When the enemies of Islam realized they had been stopped in their tracts, they decided they would kill the Prophet (pbuh), and called on any able-bodied men to come forward for the task. One of these men was Umar (ra), who was not yet in the fold of Islam, and the Muslims with the Prophet (pbuh) were alarmed, but Hamza merely said, "We don't care. Let him come. If he is coming in sincerity, then that is well and good. Otherwise I shall strike off his head with his own sword."

Hamza showed his belief in the teaching of Islam, that there was no discrimination on the basis of race, color, wealth, or status, and became like a brother to the Prophet's (pbuh) slave, Zaid. They became so dear to one another that when they went out of town, they appointed each other as heir to their fortunes and family.

Hamza was the first to receive the banner of Islam in the battle of Badr, and vanquished the strongest champion of the Quraish, fiercely fighting with the pair of swords he wielded and a symbolic single white feather on his massive chest. The enemy could not match the bravery and intensity of the Muslims that day, and turned on their heels to run.

The Quraish were bent on revenge for Badr, and gathered an army of such strength, they felt confident of victory, but the Muslims brought to the battle of Uhud a weapon that would not be defeated, a giant of a man who was fighting for the sake of Allah, and would not give up. Hamza killed many a prominent Quraish that day, and any challenge was met with a strong arm.

The Prophet's (pbuh) sadness knew no bounds when Allah's decree for his uncle was realized by the spear of Wahshi, the Ethopian slave. Wahshi in his own words describes what happened, "I am an Abyssinian man and threw spears like the Abyssinians. Rarely did I miss my target. I was told that I would be set free if I killed Hamza. At the battle of Uhud, I searched until I found a man the size of a camel, slaying every enemy he met. I hid and waited for him to come nearer. I threw at him, hitting my mark, and he stumbled towards me, but fell before he reached me. After he died, I removed my spear and reported to the Quraish what I had done. They checked my story, and then gave me my freedom, as promised."

The Quraish mutilated Hamza's body almost beyond recognition, but to avoid any revenge for this on the part of the Muslims, Allah revealed this verse, (16:126) *"And if you punish an enemy, O believers, punish with an equivalent of that with which you were harmed. But if you are patient – it is better for those who are patient."*

Hamza's sister came to the battlefield with two sheets for her slain brother, but she saw that the martyr who died next to Hamza had no burial shroud, so, they used one for him and the other for Hamza. The chief of the Martyrs in Paradise was shrouded with a sheet too small for his massive bulk. The sheet was pulled over his head, and leaves and grass were placed on his feet. The Prophet (pbuh) then led the prayers for this most courageous Muslim.

The loyalty of Hamza opened doors that were closed before, and allowed Islam to flourish. The companion Ka'b ibn Malik said of Hamza:

"My eyes weep
and they have a duty to cry
but, crying is of no benefit
The peace of your Lord from Paradise be upon you
In it is pleasure that will never cease."

~~~

From the characteristics of the Companions was their reason and understanding that brought affection, calmness, quietness, and dignity to themselves and those around them.

Qataadah (rahimAllah) said, "Men are of three types: A man, half a man, and no man. The "man" is the one from whose opinion and intelligence there is benefit. The "half man" is the one who questions

Unearthing Hidden Jewels

the intelligent and practices according to their opinion. The "no man" is the one who has no intelligence, nor opinion, nor does he ask anyone else."

Wahb ibn Munabbih (rahimAllah) said, "Whoever claims to be intelligent, but his attention is not geared towards the Afterlife, then he is a liar."

BRINGING IT FORWARD TO TODAY

We can all take a lesson from Hamza (ra) by protecting the *deen*. The best way to do that is to be like the Prophet (pbuh) in all things. If the people around you see good, then all the untruths they hear will fall away. If you are kind, then you encourage others to be kind. This takes intelligence – the kind of intelligence that will help get us to the Paradise and true rest.

May Allah guide us to this…

Did You Know?

The Chicago World's Fair of 1893 had in its "World's Parliament of Religions" a replica of a Cairo Street put on display. Once inside the gates of the pavilion, there was an exotic array of shops and houses, a café, a mosque, two obelisks, a "Temple of Luxor," and a theater that caused a rage where the belly dance was performed.

The Chicago World Fair of 1893

In the Turkish Quarter down the street, there was a mosque built with two minarets, and the call to prayer was performed

Loyalty

5 times daily, announcing the Ottoman presence on the long Midway. The mosque was graced with a gilded dome 60 feet high and a 135-foot minaret. The Sultan of Turkey, Abdul Hamid II, felt so strongly that Muslims attending the World's Fair should have a place to worship that he personally put out part of the money to build it.

One of the earliest documented Islamic calls to congregational prayer in the history of the United States took place in 1893, in conjunction with the World's Fair in Chicago. On Union Square in the heart of New York City, John Lant, a Muslim affiliated with Mohammed Alexander Russell Webb, an early convert to Islam, leaned out of a third-story window on the square to give the call that Sunday. Here is the article written about it in a New York newspaper:

NEW-YORK'S FIRST MUEZZIN CALL.

Mr. Lant Uses a Third-Story Window for a Minaret.

For the first time in New-York's history, cosmopolitan as the city is, the melodious call of the Muezzin, celebrated by every traveler in Mohammedan countries, was heard yesterday morning.

At 11 o'clock, Mr. Lant of Tarrytown on the Hudson, who, like Muhammed Alexander Webb, is a devout follower of Islam, dressed in the picturesque robes prescribed by the Moslem ritual, leaned out of a third-story window in the Union Square Bank Building at 8 Union Square and chanted in the language of the Koran the call to prayer. At its sound, the Sons of the Faithful, who were collected in a rear room, fell on their knees and bowed their faces to the floor.

The words of the call, as chanted from the minaret of every mosque in a Mohammedan town by the Muezzin, who is usually blind, run as follows: "God is most great; there is no God but Allah, and I testify that Mohammed is Allah's prophet. Come to prayer! Come to security! Prayer is better than sleep."

After the prayer, the first meeting of the Society for the Study of Islam was held. Emin L. Nabokoff was the principal speaker. He made an address, which was followed by a discussion on the topic "Islam in America." Several Mussulmans who are stopping in the city after visiting the World's Fair, were present at the meeting.

The Dawn of Islam

"O you who have believed, fear Allah and be with those who are truthful in word and deed." {The Qur'an, 9:119}

If you want wisdom, you run to the mountains. They have existed long enough to have seen all things, and their penetrating roots deep in the earth keep them from shifting to and fro with any misgiving winds that might blow their way. If you want peace, you run to the unruffled, placid pond and sit by the grove of steadfast pines keeping watch over it. If you want trustworthiness, you reach for the majestic planets. They can tell you about constancy and being drawn to that illuminate force which keeps them in orbit around it.

The loyalty of this companion was essential for the nurturing of Allah's *deen* on this earth.

Khadijah bint Khuwaylid

Quote: *"A friend is someone who walks in when others walk out."* –Walter Winchell

This noble woman was chosen by Allah to be the original "Mother of the Believers." Her caring nature gave warmth and support to Muhammad (pbuh), the best of mankind through the worst of his life.

Her father was a popular leader in the tribe of Quraish, and a successful business man. When he died in a battle, Khadijah took over his business, and followed in his lucrative footsteps.

Khadijah had good character and was so kind to the poor and her relatives in need that she earned the title of *Al-Tahira* or the Pure One.

She was always on the lookout for a man who could do her trade caravans for her, and when she heard about Mohammad (pbuh), she hired him as the caravan leader. He and one of her servants went to Sham with her goods and Muhammad (pbuh) did very well in his trade for her. When he returned, she was pleased with what he had done and sent him again to trade for her in Tihama in the southern Arabian Peninsula. Muhammad (pbuh) said of Khadijah, "I have never seen such a giving and generous employer as her. Not once did my partner and I return without finding some savory food with which to replenish ourselves."

As time went on, Khadijah was so impressed with his character and honesty that she sent her friend Nafisa to ask him to marry. Nafisa said to him, "Oh, Muhammad, what keeps you from marrying?"

"I cannot afford it," was his reply.

Nafisa then made the offer, "What if that problem was solved, and there was an offer to marry the epitome of beauty, wisdom, and nobility?"

"Who is she?" he asked.

"Khadijah," she said.

Interested, he asked, "How would this be possible?"

Nafisa replied, "Leave it to me."

Many men were inquiring about marriage to Khadijah. They knew of her looks, pleasing personality, and wealth, and knew that it would only add good to their lives to share it with her. She wanted something else, and with her next communication with Muhammad, he said yes, and the blessed marriage began. She was 40 years old, and he was 25, and he stayed monogamous for 25 years. She had six children with The Prophet (pbuh), Qasim, Abdullah, Zaynab, Ruqayyah, Umm Kulthum, and Fatima. Qasim and Abdullah died in childhood.

She became completely devoted to him, and he to her. She tried to please him in everything, so when she saw the love Muhammad (pbuh) had for her slave, Zaid, she gave him as a gift to her husband. He immediately freed him and adopted him as a son. The household grew with goodness when Muhammad's (pbuh) young cousin, Ali, came to live with them.

She accepted her husband's habit of going up to Mount Hira for retreat from time to time. She made sure he had all he needed to be well taken care of for the few days he would be gone.

In their 15th year of marriage, Muhammad (pbuh) was up on the mountain for his usual retreat and meditation when the Angel Gabriel came to him and squeezed him three times, commanding him to read.

This experience unnerved Muhammad (pbuh), and when he left the cave, Gabriel was on the horizon. He was so shaken that he ran down the mountain and home to Khadijah. He asked her to, "Cover me up! Cover me up!" When he calmed down he told her what had happened and she immediately consoled him, telling him that he was a good and kind man of peace. He never lied and he carried the burdens of those around him, and her soothing words assuaged his fears.

She took him to see her wise cousin, Waraqah, and he confirmed that Mohammad (pbuh) had, in fact, seen the angel Gabriel and that he was the Prophet spoken about in the Torah and Injil.

She was the first person to embrace Islam, becoming contemplative and finding peace in prayer, and she was the Prophet's (pbuh) support for his tough road ahead. The greetings from her Lord and Gabriel did not puff her up. She was humbled when she heard it, and honored, and replied, "Allah is peace, and from Him comes peace, and upon Gabriel I wish peace."

This woman of the Quraish was persecuted along with the small band of Muslims brave enough to proclaim their faith.

There was a boycott of the Muslims by the Quraish, and this lasted 3 years. During this time the Muslims sometimes didn't eat for days and this trial weakened the 65 year-old woman, and she died. This was three years before the Hijrah, and The Prophet (pbuh) called it his "year of sorrow", having lost his wife and protecting uncle in the same year.

Khadijah had given almost 25 years to her husband and his cause of Islam, and this "mother of the believers" bore Fatima, one of the four best women of Paradise, and was grandmother to Hassan and Hussein, foremost of the youths of Paradise. She held herself up with dignity under the pain of losing both of her sons from Muhammad (pbuh).

The Prophet (pbuh) missed her so very much and always spoke of her in the most glowing of words. He used to say, "I have not yet found a better wife than her. She had faith in me when everyone, even members of my own family and tribe did not believe me, and she accepted that I was truly a Prophet (pbuh) and a Messenger of Allah. She converted to Islam, spent all her wealth and worldly goods to help me spread this faith, and this, too, at a time when the entire world seemed to have turned against me and persecuted me. And it is through her that Allah blessed me with children."

She truly was the epitome of beauty, nobility, kindness, loyalty, generosity, and courage.

May Allah bless her and bring her peace within the hollowed-out pearl He made ready for her, ameen.

~~~

From the characteristics of the Companions was their having good behavior to all. They were good to everyone around them and anyone they had contact with during their day. This included the young, old, relatives, and those with knowledge. They would also witness their own deficiencies and the righteousness of others. The Prophet of Allah (pbuh) said, "I have only been sent to perfect righteous manners."

Bakr ibn 'Abdullah al-Murzani (raheemAllah) said, "If you see someone older than you, then respect him saying, 'He has beaten me to Islam and righteous action.' If you see someone younger, then respect him, saying to yourself, 'I have beaten him in sins.' If the people honor you, then say, 'That is from the grace of Allah, but I do not deserve it.' If they degrade you then say, 'This happened as a consequence of a previous sin.' If you throw a pebble at your neighbor's dog, then you have harmed him."

Loyalty

BRINGING IT FORWARD TO TODAY

There are so many lessons for the women of Islam today – love, loyalty, support, nobility, perseverance, generosity, kindness, purity, goodness, humility – the list of what we can learn from this gracious women is immense. The men can also get lessons from Khadijah by wanting all of the qualities above when you marry, and encouraging piety and modesty, which is sure to lead to purity in your wives and children. It's never too early to put in your mind what kind of sister you will choose to be the mother of your children…choose well, as this will give strength to the *Ummah*.

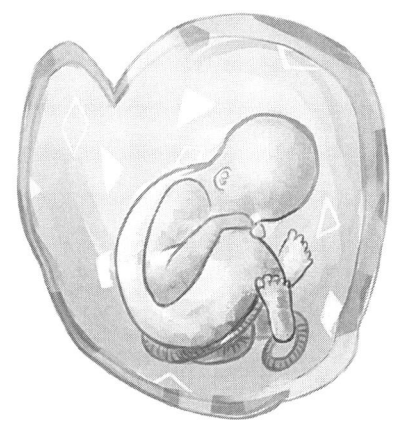

Did You Know?

The Qur'an describes the phases of the fetus in the womb, perfectly coinciding with the scientific knowledge gleaned since the microscope was discovered in the 17th century, although the Qur'an was revealed 10 centuries earlier. In Surah 32:9 the Qur'an says: *"He gave you ears, eyes, and heart, yet you are seldom thankful."*

Scientists have confirmed that the inner ear of a fetus develops first, then the eyes, and then the brain and heart.

Keith Moore was a famous Embryologist whose book about the subject was taught in Medical schools around the world.

In his foreword for the book he stated that nothing was known about the fetus before the discovery of the microscope in the 17th century. A scholar in Yemen challenged him to "come and learn about the Qur'an and what it says on this matter". Dr. Moore agreed to the meeting and was amazed at what he heard. He proclaimed that this Qur'an could only have come from God, and afterwards changed the foreword of his textbook, and how he thought and spoke about the information in the Qur'an that he learned in Yemen.

Sacrifice – Surrender of Desires

"...and that there is not for man except that which he strives for, and that his effort is going to be seen. Then he will be fully rewarded for it, and that to your Lord is the final goal."
{The Qur'an, 53:39-42}

Let's say that you are on the road to a town called 'Pleasure'. You are cruising along and come to a crossroads of sorts. Both signs say Pleasure, but one road is a short distance and the other very long. You decide to take the short route and go left, and it is a throughway where you are able to put it in gear and practically coast until you reach your destination. With very little effort along the way, you will feel the satisfaction of "arriving" to your goal, but as you begin to take in the sights, you realize something is missing. This town of pleasure is all mirrors, reflecting only desires, and, "Hmm," you think, "it's much smaller than I thought." You drive to the border very quickly and pleasure ends...

Now, if you had gone right at the crossroads, you would have seen many curves, with no knowledge of what is around them, many mountains that seem insurmountable, and pitfalls of doubt through it all. You decide to try it and haltingly begin the rocky "road less traveled", and each time you face a challenge, you think, "I must go back to the shortcut," but, just then you spy a rest area. It is a pool surrounded by palm trees tucked away where only those who strive on the path can see it. It is beautiful and beckoning you onward and you rest awhile and begin the next leg of your arduous journey. After what seems like a lifetime of this, you finally see your destination in front of you. This time the town is radiant, vast, enchanting, unending, and filled with light. You drive for what seems like eons, and your sight is rewarded with visions so pure and satisfying that you are grateful you endured the path to get there. Reward is commensurate with effort. Sacrifice begets the pleasure of Allah.

This companion is flying around Jannah with magnificent wings to replace the arms he gave willingly…

Jafar ibn Abu Talib

Quote: *"The one who has no control over his desires has no control over his mind."* – Ali ibn Abu Talib

Ja'far was the brother of Ali ibn Abu Talib, and was a first cousin of the Prophet (pbuh). The Prophet (pbuh) lived with Abu Talib after the death of his grandfather, and both boys, Ali and Ja'far grew very close with him. Ja'far was very like the Prophet (pbuh) in looks and manners, and the Prophet (pbuh) loved Ja'far for his virtues, and this love was reciprocated. Ja'far was called the 'Father of the poor' for his deep and tender caring for the less fortunate around him. One day, Abu Talib saw Ali and the Prophet (pbuh) praying so beautifully, he told Ja'far to go and join them, and so Ja'far was one of the first to embrace Islam.

Ja'far was persecuted along with all the early Muslims after the death of Abu Talib, and so was ordered to lead the immigrants to Abyssinia. The Muslims were told that the King there, Najashi, was a just one, and that they would be safe in his lands. A group of Quraish

Sacrifice

pagans went to Abyssinia to bring them back, and told the court, "A group of our misguided youth have forsaken the religion of their ancestors, and have embraced a new faith." We wish to bring them back to Makkah. Najashi was intelligent and fair, and so wanted to question the immigrants before he granted the request. He brought them to his court, and asked what new religion they had embraced that took them away from their ancestors. The Muslims had decided before they left for the court that they would have Ja'far, the eloquent one, do the speaking for them. Ja'far said, " 'O King! we were plunged in the depth of ignorance and barbarism; we adored idols, we lived unchaste, we ate the flesh of the dead, and we committed evil, we disregarded every feeling of humanity, and the duties of hospitality, and our neighborhoods were neglected; we knew no law but that of the strong. Allah, through His Mercy, raised among us a man he chose to be a prophet. We knew him well as truthful, honest, and pure. He called to the Oneness of Allah, and taught us not to associate anything with Him. He forbade us the worship of idols; and he enjoined us to speak the truth, to be faithful to our trusts, to be merciful and to regard the rights of the neighbors and kith and kin; he forbade us to speak evil of women, or to eat the substance of orphans; he ordered us to flee from the vices, and to abstain from evil; to offer prayers, to render alms, and to observe fasting. We have full faith and trust in him, and do not associate anything with Allah. We came to know the lawful and unlawful. For this reason, our people have risen against us. They have persecuted us in order to make us forsake the worship of Allah and return to the worship of idols and other abominations. They have tortured and injured us, until finding no safety among them, we have come to your country in the hope that you will protect us from oppression."

Najashi listened intently, and then requested Ja'far to recite some verses from the "book revealed to your prophet". Ja'far slowly recited some verses from *Surah Maryam*, and Najashi, with tears in his eyes said, "By Allah, I will never hand over the Muslims to you."

The Quraish tried again the next day by telling Najashi to ask what the Muslims thought of Jesus Christ. Again, Ja'far stepped forward, and without fear of reprisal, said, "We believe in Christ as the Prophet (pbuh) of Allah and His word."

Najashi picked up a piece of straw and exclaimed, "By God, the Christ, son of Mary, is nothing more than what you said, not even to the worth of this straw."

Ja'far's courage and fluent recitation was instrumental in allowing the Muslims to stay safely and securely in the land of Abyssinia for years to come.

Finally, the immigrants were allowed to return to Madina, although Ja'far was asked to remain behind. He missed his Muslim brothers and sisters very much, but did as he was told. Finally, after the victory at Khaibar, he was allowed to leave to come home, but not before converting many of the Christians in Abyssinia to Islam. Ja'far was greeted affectionately by his cousin, the Prophet Muhammad (pbuh). The just and beautiful Najashi, who also became close with Ja'far, was blessed to have the "prayer of absence" of the Prophet (pbuh) on him after his death in Abyssinia.

Sacrifice

In the eighth year after Hijrah, Ja'far and Zaid were at the head of the three thousand Muslims sent to Mauta in Jordan. The battle was fierce and bloody, taking many lives with its fury. When Zaid was martyred, Ja'far gallantly and bravely took up the banner of Allah, and broke through the enemy ranks. He felt burdened by his horse, and so he jumped to the ground and held the banner firmly in his right hand until the enemy cut his right hand off. He then grasped the banner with his left hand, until his left arm was cut off. He did then the only move left for him, he clutched the banner of Allah to his chest and sacrificed his life in that position. The companions who found his body said he had over 90 wounds, but none were on his back. The Prophet (pbuh) was receiving news of the battle through revelation and knew that his beloved Ja'far had been martyred.

The Prophet (pbuh), after Ja'far's death, was told by Gabriel that this steadfast and caring companion was given wings by Allah to replace his arms, and that he was flying about in the eternal gardens. He was lovingly referred to throughout Islamic history as *Ja'far Tayyar*, Ja'far the Flyer.

What words of praise would he have for the "sacrifice" of his two limbs now?

~~~

From the characteristics of the companions was that they would belittle their actions with respect to reward, and would never think that they had fulfilled an atom's weight of the rights of Allah.

One of the Companions said, "The rights of Allah are heavier than His slave can carry, and His blessings are more than His slave can count, so enter the morning repenting, and enter the evening repenting." The Companions reached such a level of soundness in their *deen* that if it was said to them that the Day of Reckoning would be occurring the next day, there would be no change in their state of mind.

They gave all in the sake of Allah, and the sake of their Hereafter.

BRINGING IT FORWARD TO TODAY

In this "me" society, sacrifice has lost its meaning. We have so much at our fingertips, we see no need to give anything up. We don't see that every ounce of sacrifice is worth a ton in the eternal life. Let's see how we can "give to get". Next time your cell phone starts looking a little shabby, take the money you would have spent on a new one and give it to the poor. That old phone will have more meaning and purpose, and who knows, Allah might bring you something better for your deed. If not, that small deed may be there, tipping your scale to the good, on the Day of Inevitable Truth.

Come on, let's sacrifice our two arms for the sake of Allah by reaching out to those in need – tutor, feed, comfort, pray – there are so many ways to do good with these blessed limbs we take for granted.

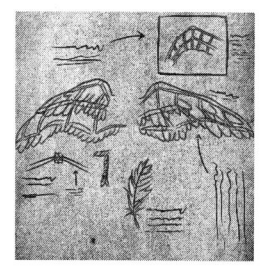

*D*id You Know?

Leonardo DaVinci designed a parachute in the 15th century. The Wright brothers took what was believed to be the first flight ever on December 17, 1903.

These attempts are the most famous and were considered at the time to be revolutionary, but let's dig a little deeper.

We rewind to the 8th century. Abbas Ibn Firnas of Andalucía, Spain, 62 years of age at the time, designed a cloak from bamboo, silk, and feathers, and jumped off a mountain, soaring like a bird for, some say, 10 minutes or so. This success story never made it to the American history books, but, nevertheless, it is well documented. It is also documented that after this buoyant, exhilarating aerial display, Firnas remembered a most important point. He forgot the mechanism to land, and without the perfectly designed tail feathers of the birds he was trying to emulate, he landed so harshly that he broke several bones. He suffered with pain for the rest of his life.

During the design phase, in his personal ledger he wrote: "What man-made machine will ever achieve the complete perfection of even the goose's wing?"

A chemist and physician, among Firnas's many accomplishments was an artificial weather simulation room, the discovery of how to facet crystal, a water clock, the manufacture of glass from sand to produce silica and quartz glass, the design of a chain of rings that could be used to display the motions of the planets and stars, corrective lenses, and a metronome. Libya honored him with a postage stamp, he has a crater on the moon named after him, and Rolls Royce made a Firnas edition with flight motifs on the hood, seats, and windows.

The Well of Good

"Say, [O Muhammad], "If your fathers, your sons, your brothers, your wives, your relatives, wealth which you have obtained, commerce wherein you fear decline, and dwellings with which you are pleased, are more beloved to you than Allah and His Messenger and jihad in His cause, then wait until Allah executes His command. And Allah does not guide the Transgressors." {The Qur'an, 9:24}

Sacrifice: The giving up of a valued thing for the sake of another that is more important or more worthy.

Each time you dip into a well, cool and refreshing, it brings good and green and a peaceful satisfaction. The well gives up, and this "giving up" provides the elixir of humanity, the lifeblood of civilizations. The well doesn't fear to give all it has, for it knows it is fed again by the movement of rain through the filtering purity of the rocks and minerals surrounding it. This brings an unbroken circle of provision. The well gives up a portion of its precious liquid to nourish and replenish, only to be revived with the influx from below. Sacrifice begets sacrifice, if the heart is pure, fearing only Allah, and unyielding to its longings.

This companion went from disbelieving idolater, to devoted believer, to elated martyr.

AMR IBN AL-JAMUH

Quote: *"Are you content that your life span comes to an end, while your religion is deficient and your property is abundant?"* – Imam as-Sajjad

Sacrifice

Amr ibn al-Jamuh was a chief of the tribe of Banu Salamah, and he was known for his nobleness and generosity. He began as a pagan, complete with an idol in his home, which he spoke to, made sacrifice to, and rubbed with oils. Amr was 60 years old when Islam came to Yathrib through Mus'ab ibn "Umayr who converted Amr's three sons. They, in turn, converted Amr's wife without him knowing it. She suggested to Amr that he listen to what his son had learned from Mus'ab, and he said he would listen. His son came to him and recited Surah al Fatihah, and Amr exclaimed, "How righteous and beautiful this speech is. Are all the teachings like this?" His son answered in the affirmative, and asked if he wished to pledge himself to Islam. Amr said he needed to consult his idol first, and his son reminded him that Manat, his idol, was a piece of wood that could neither think nor speak. Amr was adamant about asking it, though, and as was his custom, stood before the idol and asked what to do. He, of course, received no answer and so thought that Manat was angry with him, and left this "piece of wood" for a few days. His sons wanted to break him of this pagan habit so they took the statue and threw it in the garbage dump, and when Amr went looking and found it, he cleaned it up and oiled it and put it back in its place. His sons took the idol at night again and again and threw it in the pit, and each time Amr would retrieve it and clean it. One night he went to Manat and hung a sword on the statue saying, "If you are worth anything, then defend yourself tonight." The sons came and removed the sword and tied the statue to a dead dog and then threw it in a ditch filled with filthy water. When Amr found the statue this time, he left it saying, "I swear by Allah that if you had been a deity, you would not have ended up like

Unearthing Hidden Jewels

this." Not long after this, he entered Islam, and when he found the peace of Islam he regretted so much every moment he spent as an idolater. He placed himself, his sons, and his wealth in the service of Allah and His Messenger.

Amr was exempted from the Battle of Badr because of his lameness and reluctantly stayed home. Just before the battle of Uhud, he saw his sons getting ready for combat. After watching their desire to fight in the way of Allah and die as martyrs, he wanted to go with them. Now, Amr had a crippled leg, and he was elderly, so his sons agreed amongst themselves, for his own protection, that they would stop him from going.

"Father," they pleaded, "Allah has exempted you from war. Why would you want to do something that you have been excused from?"

Amr became angry then, and went to the Messenger of Allah.

"My sons wish me to stay home because I am lame. I swear, I wish to limp all the way to the Paradise!"

The Prophet (pbuh) told the sons to let him go, that maybe Allah has destined him to be a martyr. When Amr finished saying a final goodbye to his wife, he raised his hands in supplication and said, "Oh Allah! Please grant me death as a martyr, and do not bring me back here in disappointment."

In the heat of the battle many Muslims scattered from around The Prophet (pbuh), but Amr ibn al-Jamuh was seen in front, standing on his good leg saying, "I long to enter Paradise, I long to enter Paradise." He and his son beside him fought bravely until they both fell in battle, one after the other. The Prophet (pbuh) came after the battle and said,

"Don't wash them and leave their wounds, for I will testify on the Day of Resurrection as to how they died. Any Muslim who suffers a wound for the sake of Allah will come on that day with the blood transformed into a beautiful color, with the smell of the most precious of perfumes."

The Prophet (pbuh) then said he saw Amr walking perfectly on two good legs in the Paradise.

Amr came a long way, and his journey is not over yet. May Allah bring light to him in his grave.

~~~

From the characteristics of the Companions was that they had a deep fear and awe of Allah, the Most High. This fear and awe would cause them to get lost in thought and sorrow about their sins, and be completely unaware of their surroundings.

They were familiar with the saying of The Prophet (pbuh) that a man continues to do the actions of the people of Paradise until there is only an arm's length between him and Paradise, but his book precedes him and he does the actions of the people of the Hellfire and then enters it. How many boats approach a safe harbor, but when they are about to dock, a wave comes over them and they founder. All worshippers are at risk of this gravest of endings.

The Prophet (pbuh) said, "The hearts are between the two fingers of Allah. He turns them as He wishes."

Bringing it Forward to Today

The companions are sometimes simply names to us. We know very little about them, and don't realize the tremendous sacrifice done

Unearthing Hidden Jewels

in Allah's sake. Let's travel together from story to story like a bee, gathering the pollen of their righteous lives of goodness and kindness, and make honey for our time here with their richness. There once was a woman with four sons, all of whom were martyred. She praised Allah, and asked that she be united with them in Paradise. This is the true healing of the heart.

Did You Know?

During the Caliphate of Harun al-Rashid and his son, Al-Ma'moun the House of Wisdom in Baghdad got its start. It included Muslim, Christian, and Jewish scholars in its ranks, and the ancient works of the Greeks and Indians were translated into Arabic, embellished, expounded on, and then translated into Latin. This infusion of knowledge brought much-needed light to the Dark Ages of Europe.

This House of Wisdom included translators, scientists, scribes, authors, astronomers, men of letters, copyists, and the scholars needed to bring order to the knowledge being acquired. The languages spoken there were Arabic, Farsi, Hebrew, Aramaic,

Syriac, Greek, Latin, and Sanskrit. There were lively discussions, dialogue, and discourse every day. The King of Sicily, upon request of the Caliph, sent the contents of the Sicily library to Baghdad, and one hundred camels from Khurasan brought incredible handwritten books of the wisdom of that area.

This is referred to as the "Golden Age of Islam", but the Mongol invaders came in 1258 C.E. and destroyed this wonder of the time by throwing all of the books into the Tigris River. It is said that the river turned black for days on end from the ink of knowledge spilling into it.

UNEARTHING THE CHERISHED CORE

"Say, Indeed, my prayer, my sacrifice, my living and my dying are for Allah, Lord of the worlds." {The Qur'an, 6:162}

Who doesn't love to receive a beautifully wrapped gift. It calls to us with the promise of bounty and celebration, with its shiny, translucent skin encasing a treasure of unknown origin and worth. You reach to embrace it longingly, caressing the silky ribbons fashioned so carefully into a thing of ornamentation. You pull at the tie and it gives way, and suddenly you are tipping back the cover only to find another layer needing to be pulled away, and another, and another until finally you come to the jewel at the center. That's when you realize the fleeting enjoyment of the worldly packaging compared to the eons of time needed to perfect the glistening gem before you.

So too, this companion began with unparalleled earthly beauty, and peeled away the superfluous layers to reach the pith of his Islamic grace.

Mus'ab ibn Umar

Quote: *"When Allah wants good for one of His servants, He causes him to abstain from this world's pleasures, and causes him to gain thorough knowledge about religion, and gives him insight into the flaws of the life of this world. Verily, if the heart is refined and purified, the earth becomes too narrow for it, such that it has no choice but to rise above it."* – Imam as-Sadiq

Mus'ab ibn Umar was the beloved son of a wealthy man, and was brought up lavishly, and in a most luxurious fashion. He had the finest clothes, and the most exotic perfumes. Everything about him spoke of abundance, and the people looked at him with an appreciation for his beauty and elegance. His parents were very affectionate and caring to him, and even the Prophet (pbuh) said of him that there was no one more handsome in Makkah than Mus'ab.

One day he became curious about this new religion of Muhammad's (pbuh), and went to the place where the Muslims met. When he heard the words of the Qur'an, he fell in love with the religion. He converted on the spot, but tried to keep it from his influential mother. She eventually found out, and tried to chain him in his home, but finding that it didn't work, and seeing his fervor for the religion of Islam, she threw him out. He was tortured for his new beliefs, as all the new Muslims were. He began to be denied food and water, and suffered so much that the Prophet (pbuh) suggested that he migrate to Abyssinia where he would at least be safe. After many years there, he came back to Makkah, but no one recognized him. He was quiet and somber, and wore an outfit made from a coarse, worn-out blanket. His mother, seeing him this way, felt so much pity that she repented from her harsh treatment of him. When he came before the Prophet (pbuh), he was wearing a piece of animal skin with patches on it, and it barely covered his body.

The companions hung their heads in awe at the change in this young man. The Prophet (pbuh) said, "*Alhamdulillah*. Now the condition of the worldly people will change. This young man, who had no equal in Makkah, now has the regard for virtue and a love for Allah and His Messenger (pbuh), and this has made him indifferent to all worldly pleasures."

Unearthing Hidden Jewels

Many people in Yathrib (Madina) had accepted Islam at this time, and they asked that someone be sent to teach them their *deen*. The Prophet (pbuh) sent Mus'ab and he proved himself up to the task. On reaching Madina Mus'ab quietly went door to door, trying to convince people of the message of Islam. He spoke in a language they could understand, and quoted verses of the Qur'an until their hearts were softened to Islam. In this way, he averted many threats and converted even the toughest of hearts. Even Sa'ad ibn Muath, who was dead-set against Islam, listened to Mus'ab and the eloquence of the words caused his heart to open and he became Muslim right there and then. Sa'ad then went to his people and told them he was Muslim, and he wouldn't speak again to them until they had done the same. By the end of the day, the whole tribe became Muslim. Mus'ad asked permission from the Prophet (pbuh) to establish Friday prayers in Madina, and was given this. He proved to be the best choice for putting firm roots down in the City of Light. He was there to greet the Prophet (pbuh) with breathless excitement when he finally arrived.

When his mission there was finished, he turned his attention to *jihad*. Being a very gallant soldier and able general, he held the banner in the battle of Badr, and something very telling happened there. His brother was among the captives. Mus'ab said to his guard, "He has a wealthy mother. You can get a good ransom for him." His brother was surprised and said to him, "Your own brother?" Mus'ab pointed to the Ansari in charge of him and said, "He is my brother, not you!"

In the battle of Uhud, when the archers left their place to chase after the spoils of war, the Prophet (pbuh) was left in a very vulnerable position. Mus'ab saw this and tried to draw the attention of the enemy away from The Prophet (pbuh). They surrounded Mus'ab and attacked him with sword and spear, but he firmly held the banner of Islam in his right hand. The enemy moved forward and cut off this hand, and much like the story of Ja'far, before the banner could fall, he grabbed it with his left hand, but with another stroke of the enemy's sword, his left hand, too, was severed. He then clutched the banner to his breast, and this irritated the enemy so much that one of them savagely threw a spear at Mus'ab's chest, and he fell, reciting Qur'an as he descended. His brother saw the banner fluttering in the air, and took over, protecting it until he, too, breathed his last.

The Prophet (pbuh) recited this verse over Mus'ab's body: *"There are some persons among the devoted Muslims who kept their promise made to Allah"* {The Qur'an, 33:23}

Mus'ab ibn Umair was born into the wealthiest of families, but his shroud was a sheet of cloth too short for his body and so grass was scattered over his feet. May Allah be pleased with one who sacrificed it all for Him.

~~~

From the characteristics of the companions was their deep generosity, and comforting of each other. They did what they could to make the other comfortable. They tried to be the one who spent for the others on a journey, thereby believing the saying that "the sensible people were the ones who stored their wealth where no thief can reach it…the sky!"

Unearthing Hidden Jewels

They used to give graciously, never feeling superior to the one receiving. If someone asked them for something, they would say, "Oh, Welcome to the one who carries our provision to the Hereafter without any charge."

Bringing it forward to today

Whether you believe it or not, we all have this graciousness and forbearance in us. We might have to dig deep and put aside the acquired societal layers to see it, but it is there. Who doesn't love to be around kind, caring people? Deep reflection can bring about the truth of your situation, and adjustments can be done with the Qur'an and Sunnah. Let's bring forth good to one another.

Did You Know?

There was a department in the House of Wisdom in Baghdad for the closely related Sciences of Mathematics and Music, and music was taught in Andalucían colleges. The musical scale was developed by Al Kindi, and mathematically worked out to the octaves used today. The scale (Do, Re, Mi, etc…) was most probably named after letters in the Arabic alphabet.

From the translated treatise from Al-Kindi's 'ud tuning is this:

"Al-Kindi's 12-tone scale is the first tuning that uses identical note names to identify the tones of the lower and upper "octave." In his text, Al-Kindi specifically states that the musical qualities of tones separated by an "octave" are identical."

There was an ancient form of the harp found on the tomb walls of Egypt. The earliest 'uds had 1 string, and then strings were added as time went on. Finally the 5-string, fret system was developed in Baghdad, and a system of rhythm by dividing the string into forty equal parts. This instrument was called the "Kithaar", and was the precursor, most believe, for the guitar so popular today.

Avicenna, the famous physician, believed that music was a science and that it aided in healing.

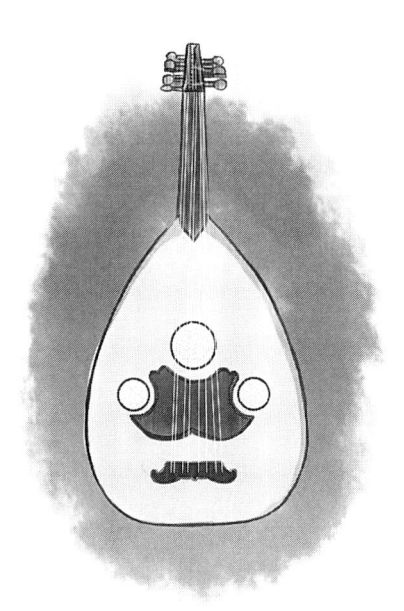

Unearthing Hidden Jewels

An Unyielding Tenacity

"But whosoever desires the Hereafter and strives for it while he is a believer - it is those whose effort is accepted by Allah."
{The Qur'an, 17:19}

A stately and lofty pine, the matriarch of her grove, had many pinecone children on her exalted branches, but there was a particularly graceful and steady daughter that gave her immense delight. The elderly pine would watch that daughter spin in the wind with her many arms wide open, pirouetting like a ballerina, dancing to the rhythm of the breeze. One morning, the mother noticed pollen glistening over her ballerina's beautiful brown coat like angel dust. She knew that soon her favorite daughter, now burst open and heavy with her own seeds, would have to leave her, but she wanted her to stay for the pleasure she brought. One day a fierce wind came to the forest. The mother began swaying and bowing with the force of the gusts; she tried, without avail, to hold onto her loved one, but knew her trunk would crack if she didn't give her up. She watched helplessly as her delicate daughter fell to earth, the impact causing her seeds to scatter, some being picked up and taken by the unrelenting wind, but one little seed staying close to the splintered and dying cone that bore her. The, now proud, grandmother watched as her daughter's seed took root, and it shot up green and beautiful, just like the fallen mother. As the years went on, her granddaughter grew larger and wider until there was not enough room for sunlight to reach them both. The grandmother was older and stronger, and the fledgling granddaughter started to fade, her tiny needles becoming brown. She was dying, and the elder knew what she needed to do. She decided to watch for the right kind of wind, and when she felt it come, she began to sway this way and that, and with each thrust of her trunk, she could feel her nobleness give way. The crack of her trunk resounded through the ancient forest, and she smiled as she saw the ground coming up to meet her. She lay next to the granddaughter and felt the warmth of the sunshine now able to reach the dying tree. The small tree grew in time and housed and nurtured many woodland creatures in her vast, open arms. The grateful grandchild never forgot the sacrifice made so she could flourish and be a boundless source of blessing to those around her.

This brave companion became a human shield, sacrificing her body for the protection of our Prophet (pbuh).

Nusaibah bint K'ab

Quote: *"Muslim women do not regard Islam as an obstacle to their progress; indeed, many may see it as a crucial component of that progress."* — John L. Esposito Dalia Mogahed, *'Who Speaks For Islam?: What a Billion Muslims Really Think'*, (p. 114)

Nusaibah bint Ka'b al-Ansariyah, also known as Umm 'Ammaarah was one of the Prophet's (pbuh) companions, and she was a great one. She was an Ansar woman, the tribe who welcomed the Prophet (pbuh) after he was forced out of his homeland in Makkah. She was one of very few women to travel with the men of her tribe and give allegiance to the Prophet (pbuh). At this, the Prophet (pbuh) said, "My blood is yours, and yours mine. Your sanctities are mine and mine yours. I am from you, and you belong to me. I am at peace with whoever you are at peace with, and I am at war with whoever you are at war with." When Umm 'Umarah returned to Al-Madinah after taking this oath of allegiance, this "War Pledge, she devoted herself wholeheartedly to passing on the teachings of Islam.

She used to come to the battlefield with bow and arrow, sword, and bandages for the wounded. Once, when she was helping in the battle of Uhud, she had intended to only bring water to the fallen warriors, but, in a moment of great difficulty, she turned and saw that the Prophet (pbuh) was unprotected. She grabbed her sword, wrapped her clothes tightly around her – especially her midsection- and stood right in front of him. As the horsemen would charge her, she would deftly jumped to the side, hamstring their mount, and then dispatch them as they fell. She did this over and over again, uncaring about the strikes on her body. Her only thought was to protect the Prophet (pbuh) at all costs. The Prophet (pbuh) came near her, only to see that Nusaibah's wounds were grave, and he ordered her to leave the battle, while praising her courage, and commanded that her son bandage her many wounds. As her son obeyed, and dressed her wounds, she noticed her son was also wounded deeply across his arm and was bleeding uncontrollably, and she treated him and comforted him. She then returned to the battle, and shouted out, "Pray to Allah, Oh, Prophet, that we will accompany you in the Paradise!" and the Prophet (pbuh) did so. Later in the battle, the Prophet (pbuh) pointed out to her the man who had injured her son and she struck her sword into his leg with all the force she could muster. He fell to the ground and was consequently killed by the warriors around her.

Sacrifice

Somewhere in the midst of this she was struck unconscious; Ibn Qumai'ah gave her a blow to the shoulder, her deepest and gravest wound. When the Muslims' retreat to Hamraa al-Asad was commanded, Umm 'Ammarrah wrapped herself tightly, summoned her strength, but had lost too much blood. She could not make the final retreat. They carried her all night until the break of dawn, and kept bandaging and treating her wounds. When the Muslims returned to Madina, the Prophet (pbuh) sent Abduallah bin Ka'b al-Maazini to Umm 'Ammaarah to see how she was. He did not enter his house before getting news of her. This grave wound did not heal for a year.

Umm 'Umarah took part in the Second Bait-ul-'Aqabah, the Battle of Uhud, the Battle of Hunayn, the war of Yamamah, and the Treaty of Hudaybiyah. Her skill with the sword in the battle of Uhud astonished those who saw her. She showed amazing strength when she lost a hand in the battle of Al Yamamah.

The Prophet (pbuh) later asked "Who has the capacity to do what Umm 'Ammaarah has the capacity to do? "I never turned to the right or to the left on the day of Uhud, but that I saw her before me, fighting off the enemy." The Prophet (pbuh) thought her most valiant.

Nusaibah bint K'ab was known for her uprightness, her religiosity, and self reliance. She asked many questions of the Prophet (pbuh), and one question was, "It seems to me that everything in Islam is for the men. I never see the women getting mentioned at all. Then the verse was revealed: *Verily the Muslim men and the Muslim women, the believing men and the believing women: each of them is the protector of the other.* {The Qur'an, 9:71}

Unearthing Hidden Jewels

She was asked one time, "Oh, woman of Ansar, did the women of Quraish also fight alongside their husbands?"

She replied, "I seek refuge in Allah, I did not see a one of them shoot an arrow or throw a single rock. But they had drums and tambourines which they beat, while reminding their men of the martyrs of Badr. They also had their *kuhl* (mascara) sticks. Whenever a Muslim would flee or cower from fear they would stick him and say, "Be brave, you are supposed to be a man."

Learned in the Qur'an and Hadith, she was a faithful, loyal wife, and a loving mother, showing remarkable patience and forbearance.

The Prophet (pbuh) said that her family was truly a great one, and he invoked Allah's blessings on them, and prayed that they should also be his friends in Paradise. Her son, Habeeb, was sent to give Musaylamah, the false prophet, a letter from the Prophet (pbuh). Musaylamah asked him, "Do you bear witness that Muhammad is the Messenger of God?" Habeeb answered firmly, "Yes, I do." Then Musaylamah asked, "Do you bear witness that I am Allah's Messenger?" Habeeb said, "I don't hear you." As this false prophet and liar started severing the limbs of Nusaibah's child, one by one, his answer never wavered. Death greeted this son with the oneness of Allah on his lips.

What greater sacrifice than one's own flesh, blood, and bones for the cause of Islam. May Allah answer the Prophet's (pbuh) prayer and count her among the righteous of Paradise.

~~~

From the characteristics of the companions was their sincerity in asking about each other. They wanted to make sure that those around them had food, clothing, money, shelter, and any other needs.

The words, "How are you?" have become empty words now, where the person asking doesn't wait for the response, and the person asked knows it is not sincere, so he doesn't really say how he is. One of the companions said that it was hypocrisy to ask if you weren't ready to help.

Abu Bakr was asked how he was. He replied, "This morning I enter as a lowly slave to a magnificent Lord. I enter the morning commanded by His commands." Imam ash-Shaafi'ee was asked in the morning how he was. He said, "This morning I have entered eating my Lord's provision, but not fulfilling true gratitude towards Him."

The companions were ready to repay their brothers debts and carry their burdens for them.

Bringing it Forward to Today

The Prophet (pbuh) allowed women to be women. He laid down the rules of Islam, and these women obeyed. During his time, women were warriors, nurses, breadwinners, scholars, mothers, protectors, business leaders, counselors, farmers, and the list goes on and on. Special talents were used and encouraged, and women were allowed to interact with men, with the proper decorum of modesty always in place. A natural balance needs to be struck again so we can give life to the "collapsed lung" of our *Ummah*. The education and revival of the wives and mothers of our Muslim youth will breathe life into the future generations of Islam.

Unearthing Hidden Jewels

*D*id You Know?

Astrolabes were global positioning instruments that determined the position of the sun and planets. They were used in the fields of astronomy, astrology, and horoscopes. They were also used to tell time and for navigation by using latitude and longitude calculated on their intricate surface. The Muslims used them to find the Qibla, prayer times, and starting days for Ramadan and Eid. The astrolabe, the slide rule of the Middle Ages, took its name from the Greek astrolabos, or "star-taking." It was used primarily to make astronomical measurements to find the altitudes of celestial bodies, but knowledgeable philosophers, astrologers, and sailors devised hundreds of uses for the instrument. The Islamic world was introduced to the astrolabe, and it was then fully developed there. The astrolabe was extremely valuable to Islamic society. In the 11th Century, astrolabe technology spread from Islam, through North Africa into Spain where European cultures gained access to the technology through Christian monasteries in northern Spain. Mariam "Al-Astrolabiya" Al-Ijliya lived in the tenth century in Aleppo, Syria and was a famous scientist who designed and constructed astrolabes. Mariam's father was an apprentice to a famous astrolabe maker in Baghdad, and through him she became a student. Her stunning handcrafted designs were so intricate and innovative that she was employed by the ruler of the city, Sayf Al Dawla, from 944 AD until 967 AD.

Forbearance – The Fortified Heart

"And you do not resent us except because we believed in the signs of our Lord when they came to us. Our Lord, pour upon us patience and let us die as Muslims in submission to You."
{The Qur'an, 7:126}

How to build a fortress for the soul:
(1) Choose the highest ground, keeping enemy force in full view.
(2) Make the material a resilient one, able to withstand even the most insidious of weapons.
(3) Have double walls, (i.e. the Qur'an and Sunnah).
(4) You will need a gate in this fortress with which to let goodness in, so the wisdom can be fluid, and one can know when to make peace.

No matter the assault on the outside, the fortress is impenetrable. The heart of a sound believer is the buttress when the body is violated, and faith is pain endured with certainty. Forbearance becomes the stronghold for the soul, with the pillars of faith as the garrison, encircling the heart, ever ready to defend this beating core from that which would tear it down.

This steadfast companion became the designate summoner for the best generation.

Bilal ibn Rabah

Quote: "As for one who wants constant security and victory over his enemies, and good health without tests, such a person does not know the meaning of security nor understands responsibility." (Excerpt from *'Quarry of the mind'* by Ibn al Jawzi)

Unearthing Hidden Jewels

In Islam, the noblest of people is the one who is most pious. He is to have piety in word and deed, and do that which is good and pleasing to Allah. Bilal ibn Rabah was such a person, and was loved and respected by the Prophet (pbuh) and the righteous companions. He was brought into slavery from Abyssinia, and worked in the house of a chief of the Quraishi tribe called Umayya ibn Khalaf. He grazed his master's camels by day with the sun blazing down on him, and then served food and wine by night to the household of Umayya. He was treated very badly, and wished for a better life, but had nothing to buy his freedom with.

One day, he heard of a new prophet calling people to worship Allah alone, and to treat each other as brothers. He heard that this prophet taught that all men were equal in the sight of the Creator. This prophet was calling the people of Makkah to give up the false idols they worshipped, and this was exactly how Bilal was feeling. He was made to worship sticks and stones by his master, and it never felt right. He began to think deeply about this new religion, Islam, and these thoughts brought him a peace he never believed he could feel.

He snuck away from his master's house and went to Abu Bakr to ask him if he believed in the Prophet's (pbuh) message, and when Abu Bakr replied in the affirmative, Bilal said he, too, wanted to become Muslim. Abu Bakr took him to the Prophet (pbuh), and Bilal took the *Shahada*. He then went to the Kabbah and saw the idols for what they really were, useless pieces of wood and stone. A man who heard him commenting on this fact there told his master, and Umayya was angry and went home to confront Bilal. He asked if Bilal had abandoned the

Forbearance

idols and his religion, and Bilal answered with a strength and confidence he never had before that, "Yes," he had been guided to the true faith."

When Umayya could not convince him to come back to the worship of the idols, he called for his other slaves to drag and torture Bilal by chaining and whipping him. Bilal kept saying through it all, "Allah is One, Allah is One" which made Umayyah even angrier. Bilal was tortured day after day, each agony afflicted becoming worse and worse as the days wore on. His words of faith never changed and on one hot day he was taken to the desert and a huge rock was put on his chest. As he endured this excruciating pain, Umayya stood over him and kept ordering him to give up his beliefs, but all he heard was, "Allah is One, Allah is One." He began whipping Bilal, and finally Abu Bakr heard of this cruel torture and immediately asked to buy Bilal from Umayya. Umayya at first angrily refused, but when he saw he was getting nowhere with Bilal, he finally agreed. He sold him for five ounces of gold, and said to Abu Bakr, "I would have sold him for one ounce." Abu Bakr replied, "Had you asked 100 ounces, I would have paid it," thus putting him in his place.

Bilal went to the Prophet (pbuh) and he declared him a free man. After a time, the Muslims fled to Madinah to escape the oppression of the tribes in Makkah, and Bilal was one of those who migrated with them. The Muslims built a masjid there in Quba, and Bilal was one of the helpers. Once it was finished, they were discussing ways of calling the people to pray. One suggestion was a flag to be raised at prayer time, and others said a fire, a horn, or ringing a bell like the Christians.

The Prophet (pbuh) wanted something different from the other religions, and after a few days of discussion, one of the companions came to him and said he saw a dream that a man was the one who called to the prayer with his voice. The Prophet (pbuh) had Bilal go to the top of the masjid and call the people to prayer, and as soon as Umar ibn Khattab heard this, he told the Prophet (pbuh) that he had the same dream. Bilal became the first caller to prayer, or *mu' adhdhin* of Islam. Bilal was very close to the Prophet (pbuh), and was designated to be treasurer, distributer of money, and entertainer of guests.

The Prophet (pbuh) once said that when he went on the journey to Paradise he heard Bilal's footsteps there. He (pbuh) asked Bilal, "What do you do?" Bilal said, "Nothing more than after making *wudu* I do as many *rakats* as were written for me by my Lord."

In the initial battle of Islam, Badr, Bilal fought with unheard of courage and strength. He went looking for the master who had treated him so badly, and called out Umayya's name when he saw him. They met in battle, and Bilal dispatched him easily.

Bilal fought in all the major battles, was with the Prophet (pbuh) when he entered Makkah, and accompanied him into the Kabbah to destroy the idols.

He then was asked to climb to the top of the Kabbah and make the call to prayer in his beloved Makkah.

The day of the Prophet's (pbuh) death, he tried to make the call to prayer, but his tears would not let him finish. He was asked by Abu Bakr to call the Muslims to prayer, but he told him he could not do the call again. He moved to Damascus to get away from the pain, and one night, sometime later, he had a dream that the Prophet (pbuh) was scolding him for not visiting him in such a long time. Bilal made the trip to Madina and wept at his (pbuh) grave. Omar sent Hussein to plead for him to do the call one more time, "In remembrance of my grandfather". Bilal agreed to this, but when the companions heard this familiar call, they wept. Bilal's grief was too much and he decided again that he would never go back on his decision. He died in Damascus with the hope of meeting the Prophet (pbuh) in *Jannah*.

May Allah bless this strong, gentle, devoted, and patient slave of His forever and ever. May his sweet voice grace the gardens of his Lord for eternity.

~~~

From the characteristics of the companions was their preparation to stand in front of their Lord before every prayer. Beginning with the *adhan*, their hearts would swell with the thought of the meeting, and by the time, "come to prayer" was said, they would already be in the presence of Allah. Ali ibn Abu Talib (ra) would become pale when he would make ablution, and when asked, would reply, "Do you realize in whose presence we will be?"

Prophet Muhammad (pbuh) said, "The first matter that the slave will be brought to account for on the Day of Judgment is the prayer. If it is sound, then the rest of his deeds will be sound. And if it is bad, then the rest of his deeds will be bad." – At-Tabarani

Unearthing Hidden Jewels

BRINGING IT FORWARD TO TODAY

How did Bilal (ra) endure the pain and torture of Umayya? What was it that allowed him to declare *shahada* for days on end with the excruciating methods being devised to make him recant his beliefs? It was his heart, pure and simple. Belief in the Oneness of Allah and the life to come entered and surrounded his heart, keeping it safe from diversion from the truth. How can we build this brace, this buttress against going astray? The bricks of small, quiet, good deeds done with belief in our Lord will surround our hearts with an impenetrable wall to buffer the constant input around us, repelling anything that would tear down our heart's shield. How can this minor pain we feel everyday compare to the trial of this stronghold of our *deen*. This should push us to declare with fervor and live our *shahada* each and every day.

Did You Know?

There once was a man living in North Carolina with green eyes and blond hair who believed that he was Irish American. One day he contracted a disease that is only found in Arab blood. As you might well expect, this made him want to dig deeply into his past, and what he found astounded him. He was from a little-known nationality called Melungeon. The Melungeons, he found out, were also known as the Makkah Indians, claimed to be of Native American, Portuguese, or Turkish descent, and some spoke of shipwrecked Moorish sailors who intermarried with Native Americans. Some had light skin as he did, but some had dark eyes and hair, and their skin was a dark, coppery color. They had wooly heads, high cheek bones, and were swarthy. Some colonies were reportedly already established by 1654 in the American Southeast in isolated communities in Virginia and the Tennessee border by the time of the first settlers there, and then spread to Kentucky and Ohio. They thrive to this day in very large numbers and have spread throughout the U.S. Blood samples taken from a group of Melungeons in 1990 showed no differences in DNA with Libya, Canary Islands, Malta, Cyprus, the Galician Mountains of Spain and Portugal, North Iraq and Iran, southern Italy, South American Indians, and the Turks.

By the way, Elvis Presley, and Abe Lincoln were Melungeon…

Unearthing Hidden Jewels

THE UNFLAPPABLE SOUL

"...so be patient with gracious patience." {The Qur'an, 70:5}

A placid pond is timeless. No one knows how long it has been there. No one knows how many intruders have shattered its glass-like surface, causing ripples to rush to the spherical shore, hurrying to escape the impact. No matter the size or shape, the pond takes in the trespasser, causing a tear in its normally unruffled crust, the intruder piercing the calm and causing undulating waves. The pond simply gives over the aftermath of these perfectly concentric waves to the land, returning to its enduring stillness. Soon the pond's façade is a glimmering, unbroken mantle, the picture of serenity, until the next challenge to its stoic, forbearing nature.

This tranquil and deliberate companion brought the best of his days of ignorance to Islam.

ZAYD AL-KHAIR

Quote: *"Patience is the summit of all virtues, the regulator of firmness, the support of reason, the seed of all goodness, and the means of the forthrightness."* – Abu Hatim al-Asamm

Zayd al-Khair started out as Zayd al-Khayl, which means 'the horseman', but when this mountain of a man became Muslim, our Prophet (pbuh) changed his name to something more fitting. The hadith says, "The best of you in the days of ignorance are the best in Islam, if you learn," and Zayd's actions before and after Islam bear this out. Here is a short story of his life before Islam:

Forbearance

A man from the tribe of Banu 'Amir took his family away from the drought they were experiencing. He left them in al-Hirah, asking them to stay until he came back for them. He vowed to find a way to earn money, or die trying. He set out on foot, and after a day of travel, came to a tent with a horse tied to it, and tried to take it, but someone warned him and he moved on without it. He traveled for another week before coming to a tent with a leather dome, and in hope, peered in. He saw an old man sitting there with his back to him, so he snuck in and sat right behind him. The old man didn't even notice him. As soon as darkness came, a very large man came riding up on what looked to be a stout warhorse. There was a herd of camels with him, one hundred strong. The man on the horse told one of the servants with him, "Milk a fat camel and bring this to the old man in the tent." The slave did so and set the milk down in front of the old man. He took a few swallows and left the rest. The man behind him crept up and drank the rest quickly, and when the slave returned he saw the bowl empty and ran and told the horseman, and he was pleased with this. He said to the slave to milk another camel and bring it to the old man. Again, the slave left and the old man took a few sips and left the rest. This time the man only drank half the milk, so as not to cause undue suspicion.

A sheep was then slaughtered, and the horseman roasted it and fed some to the old man until he was full, and then he and the servants ate from the rest and fell asleep. The man came out from where he had been hiding and got on the male camel's back and led him away, along with all the females, who followed him. He kept going through the night, and when morning came he checked for anyone who might have been following him, and moved forward again until the sun was well up. He looked behind him once again and saw a speck in the distance, which was gaining on him quickly. As the rider came closer, the man realized it was the owner of the camels. The thief came down from the camel and stood his ground between him and the herd he had stolen. He put an arrow into his bow, and the man on the horse pulled up at a distance from him and called for him to untie the camel.

"Never," was his reply, "I have a starving family, and I made an oath not to come back without something to sustain us."

"I am asking you again to untie the camel, or there will be dire consequences," the horseman replied.

The horseman told the man to pick one of the knots he made in the camel's rope, and the man picked the one in the center. From a distance far greater than a normal man could do this, the horseman easily shot an arrow into it, and the man knew he had to give up or die. He was told to get on the horse behind the marksman, and was asked what he thought would happen to him now.

Of course, the man believed that he would be punished severely, and said so, but the gracious horseman said to him, "How could I cause you harm when you have shared food and drink with, Muhalhil, my father, and spent the evening with him?"

When the man heard the name of the horseman's father, he immediately knew that this rider was no ordinary man, but Zayd-al-Khayl, the generous one.

Zayd assured him that he would not harm him, but took him back to his camp for a few days. The camels that the man took were Zayd's sister's, and so he had to protect them, but he gave the man a hundred camels of his own, and sent him back to his family.

This was the quality of forbearance he had before he became Muslim.

When this thoughtful man heard of the Prophet (pbuh), he took a number of leaders of Tayy, his tribe, and went to visit him. They happen to arrive just at the time of the *Khutbah*, and the beauty of the words resonated deeply with them. Zayd was so taken that immediately after the *Khutbah* he declared his *Shahada*.

The Prophet (pbuh) asked who he was, and he replied, "Zayd al-Khayl bin Muhalhil.

The Prophet (pbuh) then said, "I will call you Zayd al-Khair. Praise to Allah that he brought you such a long distance and opened your heart to Islam."

Zayd, from the beginning, felt the utmost of love and respect for the Prophet (pbuh), not even wanting to recline on a cushion in the presence of him (pbuh).

The Prophet (pbuh) said to Zayd on his first meeting with him, "I find that when someone is praised by others before I meet him, I am usually disappointed when we finally greet each other. You are different, Zayd. You have two qualities loved by Allah, deliberation and forbearance. Zayd praised Allah when he heard this, for giving him the traits that were pleasing to Him. He then eagerly asked for three hundred men so he could go and defeat the Byzantines. The Prophet (pbuh) exclaimed of the good in Zayd, and, upon hearing this, all of the men who had traveled with Zayd to meet the Prophet (pbuh) became Muslim on the spot.

Zayd was not sent to war, but sent back to his homeland, and on the way, he began to have symptoms of the "Al-Madinah" fever. He became weaker and weaker and finally died, having just converted and having all of his sins wiped away. May Allah accept this pure, and steady soul in His Paradise.

~~~

From the characteristics of the companions was their trying to counter hypocrisy by keeping their goodness even in public and in private. They didn't want anything hidden on the Day of Judgment to be exposed. They knew that the hypocrites would be in the lowest level of the hellfire, so they tempered their words even when not in the public eye. They took to heart the *hadith* of the Prophet (pbuh) when he (pbuh) said, "Whoever has the following four characteristics will be a pure hypocrite, and whoever has one of them will possess a characteristic of hypocrisy until he gives it up: whenever he speaks, he lies; whenever he promises, he betrays; whenever he makes a covenant, he proves treacherous; whenever he quarrels, he is insulting."

Bringing it forward to today

Allah is Al-Haleem, the Most Forbearing; the Prophets (peace be upon them) were *haleem*, the most forbearing of mankind, and regular men can have patience. We can strive for the next step to *haleem* by learning the qualities of forbearance – kindness, sweetness, a keen sense of observation, calmness, even-temperedness, generosity, tolerance, restraint in the face of provocation, and forgiveness. Each person spends from what he has. If he is good, he spends from this, even to answer evil. If we could embody a few of these softening traits, the others would soon follow. May the light of guidance ignite tenderness in our souls, and bring us much needed peace. The life to come is forever; may there be beauty there for all of us. Ameen.

Did You Know?

Some say coffee came from the Highland forests of Ethiopia, in the region of Kaffa (hence the name "coffee")…but, some say it was passed to Yemen by Sudanese slaves, and flourished there in the lava fields…and some say it originated in Yemen.

The story prevalent in many countries is of a shepherd noticing one day that his sheep were bounding around and playful, full of energy. He saw them eating berries from a certain bush, and tried them himself. The results were energizing, to say the least. This began the legend of *Qahwa*.

Warriors in Ethiopia made primitive energy bars of ground coffee and *ghee* to heighten aggression and increase stamina. These "power bars" are still eaten there today. In the 10th century, two Muslim Doctors, Rhazes and Avicenna made reference to coffee in their writings.

Unearthing Hidden Jewels

Coffee houses sprung up everywhere in the Muslim world; they used the stimulant as a substitute for wine, and social circles revolved around this warming drink.

Some scholars tried to ban it, saying it was an intoxicant, but it spread in the 16th century from Yemen to the Ottomans, and from there, into Europe.

Research shows that 1,600,000,000 cups of coffee are consumed every day around the globe.

No one could have imagined those 'goat' berries becoming an ocean of brown washing over the borders of the world!

The Enduring Soul

"O you, who have believed, persevere, endure, excel in patience, hold yourselves ready, and fear Allah, that you may be successful." {The Qur'an, 3:200}

Coral Reefs are composed of living, breathing creatures who are affixed to the coral and allow their bodies to unfurl upwards. As life ripples by them, they sift out and gather what they need, holding onto what is nourishing and letting go of the rest. They go with the flow, flexible, colorful, steady, waiting, an essential part of a much larger picture of the depth and vibrancy of life. What these graceful tendrils give off then adds to the stability of the reef, assuring the continued cycle of renewal the oceans bring to the planet.

Our next beloved companion was one of the most forbearing of the gatherers of the *seerah*.

Abu Hurairah

Quote: *"The core of adab toward the messenger (pbuh) is utmost submission and obedience to his commands, acceptance of the reports he has conveyed without contradicting them with false ideas..."* – Ibn Al-Qayyim

Abu Hurairah (literally, 'father of kitten') got his nickname because he was tender and caring to animals, and kept a kitten near him wherever he went. He was born in Yemen from the region of Tihamah on the coast of the red sea. He was an orphan, and was named Abd al-shams until his conversion to Islam. He was the first to respond to

Unearthing Hidden Jewels

his newly converted chieftain, Tufayl ibn Amr's call to the oneness of God. He left all he knew, with his mother and slave, and while traveling to Madina to meet the Prophet (pbuh), his slave boy ran away. He and his mother traveled on to Khaibar, where a battle was going on, and when he arrived, the slave came back. The first act Abu Hurairah did was to free this young man. Once he set eyes on the Prophet (pbuh), he rarely left his side, except to sleep. Abu Hurairah was one of the seventy people of Saffah. These were men who devoted themselves to obtaining knowledge from the Prophet (pbuh). The Suffah did not have clothes to fully cover themselves, and ate what came to them from charity. Abu Hurairah became contented with what filled his stomach, and memorized the doings and sayings of the Holy Prophet (pbuh) for the full four years he was with him. Sometimes he would lay on the ground on his stomach, or tie a stone around it to quell the hunger pains. He would ask questions of the knowledgeable men, just so they might feed him. One day, the Prophet (pbuh) found him like this, and invited him home. There, he (pbuh) found a bowl of milk given to him as a gift. He asked Abu Hurairah to go and bring the other people of Suffah, which made Abu Hurairah somewhat resentful. He felt he needed the milk to regain his strength, but did as he was told. When the others arrived, he was told to pass the bowl around until each one had his fill. He then handed the bowl, still full, to the Prophet (pbuh). The Prophet (pbuh) said, "You and I are the only ones left." Abu Hurairah, his hunger still gnawing at him, answered, "You are correct, Oh, Messenger of Allah." The bowl was handed to Abu Hurairah, and he gratefully drank until he could not drink any more, and The Prophet (pbuh) finished what was left. Gentle patience brought the best of results.

Abu Hurairah's phenomenal memory covered the fact that he could not write, and the Prophet (pbuh) blessed his memory, adding a deeper level to an already formidable mind. The Prophet (pbuh) would tell him to spread his cloak on the ground in front of him, and the Prophet (pbuh) would make gathering moves with his hands, place this in the cloak, and hand it back to Abu Hurairah. After this, Abu Hurairah never forgot anything. He used this gift to increase his knowledge and passed it on for good. He used to say that he would not have narrated a single hadith, except for these words he read in the Qur'an,

"Indeed, those who conceal what We sent down of clear proofs and guidance after We made it clear for the people in the Scripture - those are cursed by Allah and cursed by those who curse, except for those who repent and correct themselves and make evident what they concealed. Those – I will accept their repentance, and I am the Accepting of repentance, the Merciful."

This was the motivation for his devotion to narration. Many other companions were busy with the markets, and some were busy with agriculture, but Abu Hurairah stuck close to the source, and memorized what others couldn't or wouldn't. He became a narrator, and a fierce warrior for Islam, fighting for the cause of Islam all the way through the caliphate of Uthman. He was given the trusted job of Governor of Bahrain, and later, Governor of Madina. If it was not for his and other companions' leadership in the battle of Yamouk, the

Unearthing Hidden Jewels

Muslims would have been wiped out by the Romans.

Abu Hurairah went from a hired hand to a master, from no one special, to a notable scholar, one who narrated to 800 scholars and companions.

In his own words, "I grew up as an orphan, and I migrated as a poor man, and I was a hired hand to Lady Busra Bint Gazwan, and my pay was merely my food. Now, here I am, after Allah willed that I marry her. So praises to Him Who made this religion a straight guidance and Who made Abu Hurairah (ra) an Imam".

It was said by his grandson that his grandfather had a rope with two thousand knots in it, and every night he would use this to ask for forgiveness and praise his Lord.

He died at the age of 78, calling out to his Lord to be pleased to meet him, and pleasing to Him.

~~~

From the characteristics of the companions was that they stopped at every word and action, making sure it was from the Qur'an or Sunnah. They did not want to be of the innovators of the *deen*. The Qur'an says, "So take what the Messenger gives you, and stop at what he forbids you!"

Our Prophet (pbuh) said to beware of newly invented matters; that every single innovation is a misguidance. The companions reminded themselves and those around them of this most important point. If any one of them was determined to do something, and they were informed that the Prophet (pbuh) did not do this, they would

Forbearance

immediately change their minds, making their actions in strict adherence to the way of the Sunnah.

Bringing it Forward to Today

If we could listen more than we speak, our speech, when it did come, would be more "well thought out". The emotional speech that sometimes gets us into trouble would be cured. We need to listen until the other is finished having his say, and remember not to interrupt, and then respond with goodness.

Look at the accomplishment of one man who "listened with his heart". We benefit from his narrations every day, and he has set the path for us, through his narrations, to the Paradise, if we can only heed the words.

Did You Know?

Abu al-Hasan 'Ali ibn Nafi' was a freed slave called Ziryab or Blackbird (he was dark-complected) who revolutionized the golden age of civilization in Al-Andaluse. He was one of the fathers of Arabic music. He revolutionized the 'ud or lute by making it lighter and adding a series of strings to it to add depth. Here are just a few of the innovations he brought which are still used today:

The three-course meal (the saying, "soup to nuts" came from this).

He made asparagus a table vegetable and household name.

He carved crystal drink ware to replace the heavy metal ones.

Unearthing Hidden Jewels

He made the utensils for eating much smaller and lighter.
He invented a type of deodorant and toothpaste.
He advocated changing clothes for the seasons.
He developed an effective shampoo of salt and fragrant oils.
He cut bangs into a haircut, and innovated other styles of hair.
He was a poet, astronomer, geographer, musician, and singer (he memorized thousands of songs, making him a favorite in the court of the Caliphs).

These beneficial innovations brought by him were carried throughout the known world, and most are with us today.

A Heart Reined In

"O you who have believed, seek help through patience and prayer. Indeed, Allah is with the patient." {The Qur'an, 2:153}

Diamonds give a steady pleasure. When they were simply a lump of carbon, it was the constant and unrelenting pressure around them that condensed and polished them. From the darkest of material comes something so pure, smooth, and strong, these gems are sought after for the clarity and many brilliant facets they display. The more that life chips away at them, the more luminescent and valuable they become. Their beauty adds to the beauty of those who possess them.

This long-suffering companion, a jewel of tolerance and restraint, made a *du'a* that Allah answered with the best of mankind.

Umm Salamah

Quote: "If you are patient in one moment of anger, you will escape 100 days of sorrow." – Chinese Proverb

"Hind" as she was called at birth, had a noble and generous father. He provided so well for travelers, they would not even take provisions if they knew they would meet him. She and her husband were early converts to Islam, and she, when she had a child, was nicknamed Umm Salamah.

The Quraish were very angry when they heard the news of the couple's conversion, and the cruelty inflicted on them was intense. They were given permission to go to Abyssinia, and Umm Salamah left behind her luxurious past, hoping for Allah's pleasure.

Unearthing Hidden Jewels

They found peace and safety with the King of Abyssinia, and she was given the great responsibility of being the narrator of events in the court of the Negus, and conversations between him and Ja'far. but as news came to them in bits and pieces of the number of converts and the significant conversions of Hamza (ra) and Umar(ra), the couple longed to go back to Mecca, believing they would be safe there. They made the journey back and found that this belief turned out not to be true, and soon the persecution became so great that the Prophet (pbuh) allowed them both to migrate to Madina.

The Hijrah of Umm Salamah and her husband would prove to be a test and a trial for both of them. Here is their story:

Abu Salamah was leading the camel with Umm Salamah and Salamah on the camel's back. On the edge of Mecca, they ran into some men of her tribe, and they blocked the road. They said, "If you think you can leave us, you cannot take your wife away. She is our daughter!" They took her away from her husband forcibly. When her husband's tribe heard of this, they came and said, "You have taken your tribe member, but you cannot have the child. He is our child by rights!"

They then began a tug-of-war with the gentle child, and dislocated his shoulder. They roughly tore him away from his mother. Abu Salamah had no choice but to go on to Mecca and Umm Salamah's child was dragged away from her, broken and disfigured. Her tribe kept her as they would a prisoner. Every day from then on, she went to that spot outside of Mecca in the early morning and would cry and grieve until the evening. After a year of this, one of her cousins took pity on her and interceded with her relatives. He told them, "Why don't you let that poor woman go. She needs her husband and child." The family finally relented, and another group went to her husband's family and asked for her child.

When they were reunited, she wanted to leave right away before something else might happen to keep her from her husband. She got her mount ready to go and she and the child got as far as Tan'im, just outside of the city, where she met one of the righteous men who would not let her go alone.

"I will not leave you unprotected all the way to Al-Madina," he declared.

He led her camel, and when they reached a stopping point, he would make the camel kneel and then move away while she got down off the camel, and then he came back to unsaddle and tie her camel for her. He would then go a distance and sleep under a tree. He would then saddle the camel for departing, and lead the camel towards Madina. He did this every day until they came to the city of Quba outside of Madina, and he left her there safely with her husband and returned to Makkah. Umm Salamah's family was finally back together.

She was a wonderfully confident woman, and one time asked the Prophet (pbuh), "Oh, Messenger of Allah, I do not hear Allah mentioning women in the Qur'an. Then Allah revealed, *"And their Lord accepted their prayers. Never will I suffer to be lost the work of any of you, whether male or female; you are from one another."* {The Qur'an 3:195}

Time moved on, and Abu Salamah fought in the battle of Badr and then Uhud, but Uhud took its toll and he was severely wounded. This wound finally closed, but then abscessed and he needed to be nursed from his sick bed.

One day he said to his wife, "I heard the Blessed Prophet (pbuh) say that if anyone suffers a calamity and says, "We belong to Allah and to Him we will return," and then says, "Oh Allah, I seek Your reward and compensation for this calamity. Allah, grant me better than that which I have lost," then Allah in His Power and Glory will grant him this."

He lived only a short while longer. One day the Prophet (pbuh) came to visit the ailing man, and after he stepped out of the door to leave, Abu Salamah died, so the Prophet (pbuh) came back in and closed his eyes, and made a beautiful du'a for him. Umm Salamah, in her grief, remembered the du'a her husband taught her, and sincerely made this du'a. She was called the "noble widow of Arabia", and many of the companions wanted to make it right for her, so Abu Bakr proposed after her waiting period, as did Umar. She refused them both, but then the Prophet (pbuh) asked for her hand, and she at first told him of three qualities which she didn't think would please him. These three were that she was a jealous woman, she was no longer a young woman, and she had children. The Prophet (pbuh) replied, "I pray that Allah in His Power and Glory frees you of your jealousy. As for the age, I, too, am no longer young, and your children will be mine as well."

Their marriage was the fulfillment of her du'a, and she became the

"Mother of the believers"! She was an important narrator of Hadith. Male companions and the *Tabi'een* would come to her to learn their religion.

She relayed to us the sadness over the death of the Prophet (pbuh), and the wonderful Hadith about placing her hand on his (pbuh) chest the day he died, and the scent of his skin, that of musk, staying with her for weeks.

She stayed vibrant until the day she died. Al Hasan al Basri was raised in her home, and this may have helped elevate him to the lofty status he attained. She was the last of the Mothers of the Believers to die.

May we always take in and benefit from her legacy of forbearance and good.

~~~

From the characteristics of the companions was their not facing anyone with bad conduct, even when the others were hostile. Dawud (alayi as-salam) reportedly said to one of his sons, "Do not consider even one enemy too few."

Muhammad ibn Maqaatil (ra) said, "You pardon yourself if you do wrong, but anyone other than you is left unpardoned. You see in his eye a speck of dust, while you don't see the tree truck in yours.

It takes strength of faith to not retaliate when done wrong, and this skill can be refined throughout our lives.

Unearthing Hidden Jewels

BRINGING IT FORWARD TO TODAY

Let's put ourselves in Umm Salamah's trials. Would we be patient? Would we be able to go as deep as she, to find our trust that all would be okay? Yes, she wept, but grief is natural in the face of this kind of test. First her child and then her husband were driven away, and she didn't know what became of them.

Patience is a lost art unless practiced daily. Patience leads to a sound heart, and this is how we must meet our Lord if we wish to be successful in the Hereafter. May Allah bring us not just patience, but true and lasting forbearance, ameen.

Did You Know?

Cleopatra was not the only Queen of Egypt. A Turkic slave named Fatma al-Malikah ad-Din Umm Khalid Shajarat al-Durr, the 'Tree of Pearls', was a beautiful, pious, and intelligent slave owned by the Sultan of Egypt, As-Salih Ayyub. She bore his son, named Khalil, and was with him when he was ruler of Egypt for a decade. He fell ill and died, and she told the Commander of the Egyptian Army, and the head of the palace, but because the seventh Crusade was charging towards Egypt at the time, they decided to keep his death a secret. They sent a slave to his tent with food every day, and convinced the people that he was ill. When another son came back to Egypt, she told him of the Sultan's death, and turned over power of the country to the son. The son was a drunkard, and very abusive though, and the Mamluks in charge of the Army had him done in. These same people put Shajarat al-Durr in power as Sultan. She was mentioned in the Friday prayers at the mosque, and there were coins minted with her many titles on them. The Abbasid Caliph, however, would not recognize her, and insisted on a man as ruler. Her reign as Queen was only for three months, but in that short time there were two significant changes. One was that, under her rule, Louis IX was expelled from Egypt, and that was the end of the Crusaders in the Mediterranean Basin, and the other was the death of the Ayyubid Dynasty, and the birth of the Mamluk (Slave) Dynasty, which ruled for many years after that.

The end of her life was filled with intrigue, and she came to an unfortunate end. This woman who was named 'Tree of Pearls' because her father used to adorn her in dresses covered with pearls, for a short while, ruled Egypt as Cleopatra did in days of old.

COMMITMENT – ADHERENCE TO A VOW

"O you who have believed, do not take the disbelievers as allies instead of the believers. Do you wish to give Allah against yourselves a clear case?" {The Qur'an, 4:144}

Who doesn't love a cool, light breeze on a hot summer's day? This gentle breath of wind refreshes as it wafts by. What is not thought about at that moment is how pregnant this ever-present air may be. It carries dust and seeds, has pushed many a sail on the ocean, and gathers and distributes fragrance, all as it gusts over the surface of our blue planet. This same flurry that easily moves through the folds of our clothing could have been part of a hot, punishing squall that lifted tiny grains of sand from a desert, and carried them worlds away. It may have swooped down on its journey to you, and churned up the oxygen-rich layer of a stream teeming with life so dependent on this conveyance. It might have then picked up seeds heavy with new flora, becoming a fecundating wind, moving through and releasing its life-giving load on willing soil.

We benefit from the many stopovers these trade winds make. So, the next time a soft breeze ruffles the curtains beside you, whisper a word of thanks for the good it brings.

Our next companion brought much good, as our Lord's breeze of guidance moved him through his stepping stones of life.

SALMAN FARSI

Quote: *"Does one marvel at the speed of water, or something else, as it runs downhill? Rather, the marvel is in one who ascends,*

Commitment

one who carves out a path and overcomes obstacles." – Ibn Al-Jawzi

Here is Salman Farsi's story in his own words:

"I was born in a village called Jayyan in the area of Isfahan. My father was the leader of the town, wealthy, and socially high in rank. His love for me knew no bounds, so much so, that he kept me confined to the home. We were followers of the Magian faith, and I was guardian of the "sacred fire" which was worshipped. It was not allowed to go out, day or night. My father had a grain plantation he used to run, but one day a matter came up which made him not able to go to the village. He asked me to go and take charge of his matters there. On my way, I passed a Christian church and heard their voices raised in prayer. I was fascinated by this, as I knew almost nothing of other religions. I stopped and went inside to see them.

I found their prayer appealing to me, and I said, "By God, their religion is better than ours!"

I asked where this started, and they told me, "Near Syria". I didn't leave until after night came, and when I returned to my father, he asked about my day.

I told him, "Father, I went by a church, and their religion appealed to me, so I stayed all day."

My father was shocked and tried to convince me that our religion was better than this, but I swore again that their religion was better than ours. He then locked me up in my home and chained my feet.

I waited for an opportunity to send a note to the Christians to let me know when any travelers to Syria contacted them. When news came that travelers to Syria were on their way home, I slipped away, disguised myself, and traveled to Syria with them.

When I reached my destination, I asked who the best person in their religion was, and I was told of a bishop in charge of the church there. I went to him and told him that I wanted to become Christian, serve and pray with him, and he agreed, and took me in. I soon found that he was evil, ordering his followers to give money in charity, but keeping it all for himself. Shortly afterwards, he died and when they came to bury him, I told them about the gold he had hoarded, and showed them where he had buried it. The people did not bury him, but crucified and stoned his body.

They replaced him with a very pious man, and I lived and learned from this man until one day he became ill. "Who do you recommend I go to now?" was my question to him on his deathbed. He sent me to a place called Mosul, and I introduced myself to the person he recommended. He invited me to live with him, and he, too, was righteous and a good teacher. He also died, but before he did, he told me of a good man in Nassibayn. I traveled there and he was a virtuous teacher, but life ended for him soon after my arrival. I went to the person he told me about in Ammuriyah, and I lived with him long enough to gain some wealth and cattle, and when he was dying, he told me that he knew of no one who held to the good life, but that there would be a prophet coming of the Arabs, sent with the religion of Abraham, and will live in the land of date palms between two mountains. "Here are some signs so that you may recognize him," he softly said. "He will eat from a gift, but not from charity, and there will be a ring indicating the seal of prophecy between his shoulder blades. I advise you to try and find him."

I stayed for a short while longer in the town until I heard of some Arab merchants from the tribe of Kalb who were going to the Arabian Peninsula. I told them that I would give them my cattle and wealth if they would take me with them. They agreed, but between Damascus and al-Madina, they sold me to a Jewish man as a slave. After a while, his cousin bought me and took me to Yathrib, as Madina was called then, and I saw the palm trees spoken about by my companion in Ammuriyah. I knew I had to be close now, to finding the man of goodness.

I spent a long time with this owner of slaves, with many hours of grueling hard labor. One day, I was working in a palm tree with my master on the ground under it, when one of his cousins came rushing to him, distressed.

"What is the matter with you?" my master asked him.

"Banu Qaylah is welcoming a man to Quba today who claims to be a prophet!" the man replied.

Imagine my joy at hearing this; I almost fell out of the palm tree onto my master. I climbed down and asked him again what he had said, but my master struck me hard, saying, "What does this have to do with you? Go back to work!", but I would not be denied. When night came, I took some dried dates and went to the Messenger (pbuh). I thought to test him, so I told him that I had some charity for him, and he took it and gave it away to his companions, but did not eat it himself. After seeing this first sign, I went home and later brought some more dates, offering them to him as a gift. He ate along with his companions this time, and I was thrilled to see the second sign.

The next time I saw him, he was burying a companion at Baqi. He was sitting, and was wearing two garments, and I moved around him to see his back. He knew what I was looking for and lowered his cloak, and there was the sign spoken about. I threw myself on him, kissing him and weeping. He asked what the matter was, and I told him the circuitous story of how I came to him, and he was fascinated.

I found that day not only the true prophet, but a new life."

The Prophet (pbuh) told Salman to pay off his bondage, and his Jewish master asked for three hundred date palm shoots and forty ounces of gold. He didn't know how he was going to pay it, but the Prophet (pbuh) knew how valuable he was, and asked his fellow Muslims to help him to pay it off. There were many who gave three or four trees, whatever they could afford, and soon they had the three-hundred tiny majestic date palms. They all went to the garden of the Jew and The Prophet (pbuh) told Salman to dig three hundred holes and he (pbuh) would plant them himself. Salman said later, "By Allah, not a single seedling failed to thrive." The first part was done, but how could they fulfill the second? Well, one day, as Allah so willed, some gold was gotten in a battle, and it was the size of a hen's egg. Salman took it, weighed it, and it weighed exactly forty ounces. He took it and paid off his debt, and immediately went back to the Messenger (pbuh) and offered his life to Islam. A discussion soon started about whether Salman was a Muhajir or an Ansari. One side said he left his home in search of the truth, so his wanderings made him a Muhajir, and the other side claimed that he had settled in Madina before he was Muslim, and then became Muslim, so he was an Ansari. The

Prophet (pbuh) settled it peacefully by telling the companions that Salman was from his family. In that honored and enviable position, he was tied in brotherhood to Abu Darda, the wise man.

Salman missed the battles of Badr and Uhud, because he was enslaved at the time, but fought in every other battle the Muslims had. He was knowledgeable regarding the ways of the Jews, Persians, and the Romans, and was instrumental in passing on the winning strategy of the Battle of the Trench. The Prophet (pbuh) was told that an army of ten thousand warriors from Quraish and the surrounding tribes were gathering to challenge the Muslims. The Prophet (pbuh) called together his companions and made consultation with them, and that is when Salman put forth the idea of digging a trench across the accessible part of the city. This only needed to be done at the north of Madina, as the other three sides were naturally protected by orchards and volcanoes. The companions dug with simple tools as the Prophet (pbuh) worked right alongside of them, making supplication and inspiring them with his (pbuh) words. Salman came upon a rock that even his inordinate strength could not budge. The Prophet (pbuh) came over and took the axe from him, striking the rock once. Salman saw a flash of light under the axe. The Prophet (pbuh) hit it again, and again Salman saw the flash of light. After the third time the rock shattered, with that same flash of light, and Salman said, "Oh, Prophet of Allah (pbuh), what were those flashes?" The Prophet (pbuh) replied, "On the first strike, Allah granted me conquest of Yemen, on the second flash, the conquest of Shaam and Egypt, and on the third, conquest of the East." Salman knew then that the call to one God would move through the land.

The trench was finished in only six days, and the enemy had never seen such a thing as this. With the help of Allah, the enemy scattered, and victory was for the Muslims.

Salman, in other battles, delivered eloquent speeches to the enemy about becoming Muslim, and only when they refused would he attack them.

He followed the Prophet (pbuh) until he died, and then followed his ways for the rest of his life. He lived in a house so small that when he stood, his head brushed the ceiling, and when he lay, his feet hit the walls. He owned only a large bowl, a trough, and a basin to wash with. When he became Governor, he ruled over thirty-thousand people, but gave away his salary!

One day, Salman was in the marketplace, and a man next to him bought some horse feed. The man looked around and signaled for Salman to carry it for him. Salman quietly loaded it on his back and followed the man down the street. Soon, the man noticed that everyone was greeting his helper, and so he asked one of them, "Who is this man?" He was told, "Salman al Farsi." He turned around in amazement and said, "I swear by Allah, I was not aware of who you were. Give me the bags!" Salman replied with, "No, I will carry them. This has given me a chance to reflect on three benefits of helping: I stopped my pride in its tracks, I gave a hand to a fellow Muslim, and if you had not found me, you may have burdened someone weaker than me with it." When Salman was questioned about his lineage, he would respond, "I was not aware that I had a Muslim father, but I am the son of Islam." Umar loved this saying so much that he adopted it for himself.

When Salman was near death, he asked his wife to mix some water with a bottle of musk that he had, and to then sprinkle it around the bed, as he knew, "We will be visited soon by creatures not of this earth."

May Allah reward Salman Farsi for following the path he knew to be true, no matter how long it took him to reach his goal.

~~~

From the characteristics of the companions was al-Ikhlas or sincerity in knowledge and actions. They had a fear of "showing off". Ibraheem al-Taymi said, "The sincerely devoted one is he who conceals his good deeds as he conceals his bad ones."

For these companions, to have knowledge was to practice what they had learned. They would rather learn and practice than to occupy themselves with people. They would search in their actions for any pleasure at being seen doing good, and weep over this shortcoming.

Bringing it Forward to Today

Commitment, following through, keeping one's promises, being open to Allah's guidance, being persistent in one's belief…so much goodness can be gleaned from Salman Farsi's story. If you are open to it, Allah will guide your every step to where you need to be in life. When you make a vow, keep it, and move towards righteousness in all that you do. You will find that the people who disagree the least among themselves are the people of the *Sunnah* and *Hadith*.

Unearthing Hidden Jewels

Did You Know?

Ibn Sina began his illustrious study of medicine at the age of thirteen, and was a prolific writer of medical and philosophical texts, over four hundred and fifty in all.

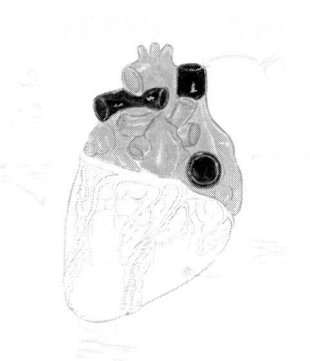

Forty medical texts have survived to today. His *'Canon of Medicine'* expounded on the works of Galen and Hippocrates of Greece, and became the standard text for many universities in medieval times. This work was a summary of all the medical knowledge known, consisted of five volumes covering everything from pleurisy to nervous disorders, and continued to dominate in this field until as late as 1650.

He also wrote many philosophical treatises which were later soundly refuted by Al-Ghazali as being on the edge of Islam.

There is a foundation bearing his name that since 2001 has been trying to help underserved families with their health care needs.

George Sarton, eminent historian of science, quoted that Ibn Sina retained his notoriety for a thousand years as one of the greatest medical scholars in history.

THE DEEPLY OBLIGING HEART

"Indeed, those who have believed and emigrated and fought with their wealth and lives in the cause of Allah, and those who gave shelter and aided - they are allies of one another..."
{The Qur'an, 8:72}

It doesn't matter in what country you experienced your childhood, in the neighborhood there was a home where all children were welcome, the door was always open, there was always food on the stove. The kids from every family on the block melded into one big adopted family. Usually the hosting family was blessed with many children themselves, and their attitude was, "So, what's a few more?" They were loving to all the children, and the children felt they could talk to them about anything, something they could never do with their own parents. This built trust in these kids, and their social skills were honed by the loving guidance and admonition they received from these "surrogate" parents. Some hearts were simply created open...

Our Prophet (pbuh) was lovingly welcomed with an open heart by this devoted companion...

ABU AYYUB

Quote: *"I learned that every mortal will taste death. But only some will taste life."* – Jalaal-ud-Deen Ar-Roomi

His full name was Khalid bin Zayd bin Kulayb, and his tribe was Banu Najjar. He was Ansari, with a nickname of Abu Ayyub, which is a name well known by Muslims. His was the home where the Prophet (pbuh) stayed when he came to Madina. Here is how it happened. When the Prophet reached Madina, everyone there wanted to have him as their houseguest, and every door was thrown open wide for him. What was he (pbuh) to do? How would he choose without hurting or alienating some followers? Our wise Prophet (pbuh) had the best solution. His camel would make the choice by stopping in front of the house where he should stay, and no one could argue with his methods. His camel seemingly meandered slowly, past all the anticipatory homes on his way, but she finally knelt down on a vacant lot across from Abu Ayyub. The Prophet (pbuh) did not dismount yet, though, and allowed her the space to move. She got up, as to move away, but then settled back down in the same spot. Abu Ayyub could not believe his eyes, and his heart leapt in his chest. He ran to get the Prophet's (pbuh) luggage and brought it into his two-story home. The Prophet (pbuh) explained that he should stay on the first floor, so as not to disturb Abu Ayyub and his family with all the visitors. Abu Ayyub agreed and all settled in to rest. Soon, though, unrest settled in on the upper level.

"What have we done?" Abu Ayyub exclaimed to his wife, "We have put ourselves above the Messenger of Allah! We have put ourselves between him and the revelation! This is a disaster!"

He and his wife could find no peace after that, and so slept against the wall, and when they did move, crept about on the edges of the floor. When morning came, he complained to the Prophet (pbuh) about his night, but the Prophet (pbuh) gently insisted this was best because of his visitors. Abu Ayyub and his wife tried it again, but one night it was so cold that a water jug cracked and water came spilling out onto the floor. He and his wife used their only blanket to sop it up before any water could drip on their esteemed guest.

In the morning Abu Ayyub told of their night, and finally the Prophet (pbuh) agreed to go to the upper level.

The Prophet (pbuh) was a valued guest in the house for seven months, the time it took to finish his masjid on the land across from Abu Ayyub's house. During that time, Abu Ayyub was blessed with witnessing Divine Revelation, righteousness, angels, and the way of prophetic worship. His home was filled with light, day and night. When the masjid was finished, the blessed Prophet (pbuh) became Abu Ayyub's neighbor.

The following story illustrates how close their friendship was.

One day the Prophet (pbuh) was pushed out of his house from hunger, only to find Umar and Abu Bakr there too, and he asked them why they came out. "We were hungry," they replied. He then took them across the street to Abu Ayyub, and, as Abu Ayyub always saved food for his beloved Prophet (pbuh), was able to feed them three kinds of dates, and a slaughtered goat, one half which was made into a stew, and the other roasted, and wrapped in wonderful bread. After they had eaten this feast, the Prophet (pbuh) exclaimed that, "All would be asked about these blessings and to give thanks to Allah for it."

In order to repay Abu Ayyub, he requested that he come to the Prophet's (pbuh) home the next day, and, of course, Aby Ayyub said, "I hear and I obey." When he arrived the next day, the Prophet (pbuh)

Unearthing Hidden Jewels

had a slave girl for him who had been helping in his home. He said for Abu Ayyub to be good to her, as she had been well-behaved with the Prophet (pbuh). Abu Ayyub took her home, and he and his wife immediately freed her.

Abu Ayyub spent his whole life in *jihad*, and it was said that he never missed a battle from the time of the Prophet (pbuh) until the time of Mu'awwiyah. He not only fought bravely, but was well trusted by the people and the rulers of his time. He was the Imam when Uthman couldn't be, and he was Ali's vicegerent when he left for Iraq. He spoke against incompetent tyrants when needed, and was an inspiration to the men he fought with.

His final wish was to be buried beneath the walls of Constantinople, a victory the Muslims had not yet won. His companions pushed the enemy hard after his death, so he could be laid to rest beneath these walls.

His grave became honored by the people of Constantinople and the Ottoman rulers.

May Allah bring him peace and a spacious welcome in His paradise.

~~~

From the characteristics of the companions was that they never believed they had caught up with thankfulness to Allah. They would see all their gratefulness as Allah's favor on them, thus making it impossible for them to catch up.

Abu Bakr ibn 'Abdullah Al-Muzani (r) said, "Never does a slave say, "*Alhamdulillah*" without more gratitude becoming incumbent on him!"

You can't praise Allah enough for your favors. Mujaahid and Makhool (r) commented on the statement of Allah, *'Then you will be asked that Day about the enjoyment...'* They said, *'Indeed, this is cool drink, shelter, a full belly, the beauty of features, and the pure joy of sleep.'*

A-Hasan al-Basri (ra) commented about the statement of Allah, "Verily mankind is ungrateful to His Lord," to mean that mankind remembers the tragedies, but forgets the blessings."

BRINGING IT FORWARD TO TODAY

Making someone welcome is an art. Some come by it naturally, but most of us have to work at it. It comes from a part of the heart that cares more for another's comfort and well-being than its own. Sometimes we feel like we are giving over something precious to our guest, when, if the truth be known, we are receiving untold blessings for each moment of comfort they feel. Let's make being gracious a goal of ours.

Did You Know?

The Golden Age of Islam fueled the Renaissance with an influx of scholarly discoveries. During the last days of the fall of Andalucía, Christian monks in Europe were hungry for knowledge. They had a mere 100 books to choose from for their studies, and knew there must be more. When they heard that Spain was taking a tumble, and the Muslim Empire was

Unearthing Hidden Jewels

waning, they set out to find out if what they heard was true, that scholars in Andalucía had 80,000 books at their disposal.

Their journeys to Spain and back were the beginning of the days of the Renaissance in Europe. They traveled to the city of Toledo in Spain, and found there universities filled with wondrous knowledge, and the brightest minds. Their insatiable intellects were filled to the brim, and then emptied out when they returned to Europe.

They found treatise on every division of Science and Mathematics, including flight, optics, medicine, capturing time, the stars and planets, and so much more. The history books still do not reflect this, but any foray into this Golden Age will bring proof of these humble discoveries.

The Duty of a Heart to its Soul

"O you who have believed, fear Allah and seek the means of nearness to Him and strive in His cause that you may succeed."
{The Qur'an, 5:35}

The sun rises from 93 million miles away, slowly lighting all that it reaches. When the sky is sated with blazing splendor, light finally gives over to light, bringing brilliance to the day unequalled.

There is beauty, nobility, warmth, and life to benefit every living thing. At the close of day, this fiery orb slowly begins its descent, holding its shape through the layers of atmosphere as they bend the prismatic hues of its wavelength, leaving only an unrelenting crimson as its garment. As this unpretentious exhibitionist slips below the horizon, it carefully yields to the twilight cover of night, putting another day to rest.

A dutiful heart drove this consummate companion to spread the beam of Islam through his whole tribe…

At-Tufayl bin ʿAmr Ad-Dawsi

Quote: *"All humans are dead, except those who have knowledge. And all those who have knowledge are asleep, except those who do good deeds. And those who do good deeds are deceived, except those who are sincere. And those who are sincere are always in a state of worry."*
–Imam Shaafiʿi

At-Tufayl was a noble Arab, one lord of his tribe, chivalrous, welcoming, protective, and poetic with the beauty of his language. He decided one day to ride to Mecca, and it happened to be the time of great strife between the Quraish and the Muslims. Each side needed, and actively sought, support from the surrounding peoples. He wandered into the battlefield, solely by accident, and the Lords of the Quraish immediately came forward to welcome him. They gave him what they thought was sound advice. "Don't speak to Mohammad, or hear anything he has to say, for he has speech that splits father and son, brother and brother, man and wife. These words of his are stronger than the strongest magic," was their cry. They told such dark and inflated stories out of fear that this noble man might become Muslim and take his whole tribe with him. After hearing their speech, At-Tufayl made a vow never to go near Mohammad (pbuh) or speak to him or hear him. At-Tufayl was on his way to the Kaaba to pay his respects to the idols, and he was in such fear of the Prophet's (pbuh) words that he stuffed his ears with cotton. As soon as he entered, he found the Prophet (pbuh) in prayer, and he watched with fascination, and was shook by the movements and feelings surrounding the one who was praying. He was intrigued, and followed the Prophet (pbuh) home. When he was invited to enter, he said, "Your people of Quraish told me so many stories about you that I stuffed cotton in my ears, so as not to hear your seductive words. It was Allah's will that I did hear, and I found it so beautiful. Teach me."

The Prophet (pbuh) recited to him *al-Ilklas* and *al-Falaq*, and never hearing anything more beautiful, he put forth his hand to the Prophet (pbuh) and took *shahada*.

After a time, he decided to go back to his tribe, and asked the Prophet (pbuh) to make a prayer for him and to give him a sign with

Commitment

which to call them. The Prophet (pbuh) said, "Oh, Allah, make a sign for him to aid him in the good deeds which he intends to perform."

As At-Tufayl neared his homeland, he came to the high ground above his home, and a light like a lantern came close to his eyes, and he asked Allah to put it in a spot more subtle, and so Allah put it on the end of his riding whip. When he reached the bottom of the trail, his aged father came to greet him. He asked him to stay away, saying, "I no longer belong to you. I have become Muslim." His father said he would follow his religion, and he told him to go and wash himself for his *Shahada*. After he finished with his father, his wife found out he was back and went to him. He told her the same thing, and she went and took a private bath, and she accepted Islam as well.

He then called his tribe together and explained Islam to them and the only member who converted, then and there, was a man known to many Muslims, Abu Hurairah.

He and Abu Hurairah traveled to the Prophet (pbuh), and the Prophet (pbuh) asked about his tribe.

"Oh, Messenger of Allah (pbuh), they are still in ignorance," At-Tufayl answered. The Prophet (pbuh) raised his hands and made a dua that all of At-Tufayl's tribe would become Muslim. He advised him to go back to his tribe, and gently call them to Islam. At-Tufayl did travel back and called them patiently and waited many years, all the way through the Hijrah, Badr, Uhud, and the Trench. He finally came to Madina with eighty families who had accepted the call. The Prophet (pbuh) was pleased, and shared booty with them. At-Tufayl asked if he and his people could have the honor of being the Prophet's

Unearthing Hidden Jewels

(pbuh) right flank in his wars, and asked that his tribe's motto be allowed to be mabrur or May Allah accept our righteous deeds.

After the conquest of Mecca, At-Tufayl watched as all the idols in the Kaaba were destroyed, and asked if he could go and destroy the idol of his tribe. The Prophet (pbuh) gave his permission, and At-Tufayl got back to his home, went right up to the idol and got ready to burn it, and the pagans around it thought, "Surely, great harm will come to At-Tufayl for this deed!" At-Tufayl was unconcerned, and put a torch to the idol, and sang a song the whole time about how worthless the idol was. By the time the last splinter was singed away, his whole tribe had become Muslim.

After the Prophet (pbuh) died, this fearless companion committed himself and his son to the Caliphate. They were part of the Muslim army that kept order by fighting the ones who wanted to leave the religion, thereby helping to preserve the Ummah. He and his son marched with the army to the Battle of Yamamah. At-Tufayl had a dream on the way that his head had been shaved, a bird flew out of his mouth, and a woman put him inside her stomach. His interpretation of this dream was that his head would be severed in the battle, his soul would leave his body, and the earth would accept his body like a mother's womb. His hope was to die as a shahid, and his son had the very same wish, but At-Tufayl believed it would not happen right away for his son. At-Tufayl was indeed martyred in the battle, but his son fought until he was wounded many times and lost a hand. During Umar's time he was invited to come to eat with the Chaliph, and he was shy to reach for food because he thought it would upset the rest of the companions. Umar said to him, "I swear, I will not taste the food until you touch it. We are not repelled, for you are the only one of us who already has a part of himself in the Paradise." In the battle of Yarmuk, At-Tufayl's son was granted death on the battlefield, and left this earth as a martyr, fulfilling his father's dream.

May At-Tufayl and his son be rewarded for their bravery under fire and commitment to the cause of Islam.

~~~

From the characteristics of the companions was their choosing their brothers in Islam carefully. They wanted to fulfill the rights of their brothers, but also wanted their rights fulfilled. They knew that any man that did less than this was not concerned with their welfare.

Iman Ash-Shaafi'ee (ra) used to say, "If it was not for conversing with brothers in this world and night prayers, I would not have preferred to have remained alive."

They would refrain from relationships with the crazy, the liar, and the corrupt one. They believed that the crazy one's silence was better than his speech, it was never comfortable to be around a liar, and that the corrupt were mostly hypocrites, and did not want to help in any religious matters.

They chose their brothers wisely.

Bringing it Forward to Today

This generous, noble, and literate man was the embodiment of the *Hadith*, "The best of you in the time of ignorance will be the best of you in Islam, if you learn."

Unearthing Hidden Jewels

His heart was true and open, and he fell in love with the Qu'ran when it reached his ears. He asked Allah that he be a martyr, and made du'a that his son also have the blessings of martyrdom. He knew that nothing but the Paradise awaited anyone who died this way, and wanted the best for his son.

What do we want for our children? Is it all "of this world"? At-Tufayl knew that the du'a he made, if granted, might mean that his son would die a violent death, but his belief in the Hereafter was so firm, he had no fear of that.

We need to fear the things of this world less, and fear our Creator more. That is where true peace lies.

Did You Know?

This gateway to the Sahara in Mali was the intellectual and spiritual capital and center for the propagation of Islam through Africa in the 15th and 16th centuries.

It was named for the old woman named Buktu who used to guard it, (tim, place of Buktu), and at one time had 100,000 inhabitants and no less than three great mosques.

Imminent scholars gravitated to Timbuktu from Cairo, Baghdad, and Persia.

The city had 180 Qu'ranic schools with 25,000 students, and sixteen mausoleums and holy public places. It was the crossroads where precious manuscripts were traded, along with salt, gold, cattle, and grain.

The Sultan of Mali, Moussa KanKan Moussa, was one of the richest kings of his time, and built the grand mosque called Djingarayber Mosque. Although this mosque, along with the other two in Timbuktu, have been restored almost constantly throughout the years, they are today under threat from certain desertification.

Two Hearts and a Shared Covenant

"Indeed, those who pledge allegiance to you, O Muhammad – they are actually pledging allegiance to Allah. The hand of Allah is over their hands. So he who breaks his word only breaks it to the detriment of himself, and he who fulfills that which he has promised Allah – He will give him a great reward."
{The Qur'an, 48:10}

Figs have a sweet aroma and are soft in your hands. Their outsides have an earthy beauty, multi-hued in its complexity. When you slice through its iridescent covering, the inside is a delight to the eye, a starburst of crimson blush, with the imprint of the generations to come sprinkled through it.

Pomegranates are also a delight to the eye. They are all decked out in apple red, a royal fruit wearing a crown. Its white-robed interior releasing honeyed jewels like caviar of the bough.

Sweet fruit begets sweet fruit, ripe, luscious, and aromatic.

Our next companion, delicate fruit of the spirit, had a special place in our Prophet's (pbuh) heart.

Fatima bint Mohammad

Quote: *"In the sight of love, fear isn't even as great as a single hair: in the law of love, everything is offered as a sacrifice."* –Rumi

This gem was the fifth child of Mohammad (pbuh) and Khadijah (ra). She was born before the revelation came, and was five years old when her father became the Messenger of Allah. She was very close to her father, but after he received revelation, she realized her deep love and commitment to him, and, even as a child, became a staunch defender of him against his enemies. She was called "The Mother of her Father", and sometimes "Al Zahra" for the illumination in her face. She witnessed numerous attacks on her father, and many times her tiny body stood to its full diminutive height and spoke out against the oppression she saw. At one point, the oppression got so bad that the Muslims were given permission to migrate to Abyssinia. She did not go, but had to say a painful goodbye to her much-loved sister Ruqayyah and, Uthman, her husband, who had decided to take the arduous journey.

At 12 years old, she was forced out of Mecca along with her family, and they lived out in the elements with little food or contact for three years. Her mother, Khadijah, died soon after they were allowed back in, and it hit Fatima very hard. Her beloved Ummi, her tender protector was gone. This was a scar that would never heal.

Fatima took over the comfort and care of her father (pbuh) after her mother's death. She rarely left her father's side, staying close through every trial.

She had fine manners with gentle speech, and she was kind. The only time anyone saw her fiery side was when she was defending her father from the tormenting of the Quraish. When the Muslims were given permission to leave for Madina, she had to, again, be torn from those she loved. Her father and Abu Bakr left on Hijra, but she and the rest of her family followed him soon after.

She flourished along with her Islam in Madina and in the second year of hijra, proposals of marriage started to come. She turned them all down until Ali, the Prophet's (pbuh) cousin, came to ask for her hand. Her father had recommended to her that she accept his offer, and so she did. A very blessed union happened that day. Her dowry was Ali's shield, which he sold for 500 dirhams. The elder companions were invited to the wedding, and all of Madina celebrated with them.

She led a very simple life after her marriage, and many times she went hungry. She was thin and frail, and worked so hard her fingers blistered, but she rarely complained. The one time she did complain, her father suggested that instead of a slave, which was the request that she brought to him, she should say the tasbieh, "Glory be to Allah, all praise is due to Allah, Allah is the Greatest" before she slept. He told her this would be more beneficial to her.

She had much sadness when her sister, Ruqayyah fell ill and died just before the Battle of Badr, but her sadness turned to joy when she heard of the victory there. When her first son, Hassan was born shortly afterwards, Ali wanted to name him Harb, which means war, but The Prophet (pbuh) suggested the name Hassan, which means goodness. Husain, her second son, followed one year later. These beautiful children were a delight to her father, and those around her. She gave the world two steadfast and righteous sons.

She lost two more sisters to illness, but made her daughters namesakes for them, thus keeping their memory alive.

During the Battle of Uhud she was bringing water and helping the wounded. When the fighting came to an end, she wept as she searched for her beloved father. She found him with several wounds, and as

Ali poured water from his armor, she washed his injuries. She noticed water made them bleed worse, so being a resourceful woman, she found a mat and burned some of it, laying it on the wounds until they stopped bleeding.

She was always active in the community, hosting the poor and caring for them. At the Battle of the Trench, she helped by preparing food and she led the women in prayer.

Fatima watched as her father (pbuh) entered Mecca victorious and felt such joy as he moved through and cleansed the Kabah of idols. Her heart almost burst with love as she witnessed him pardoning those who had oppressed him. That same year, her third sister, Umm Kalthum, died, but through this tragedy she and the Prophet (pbuh) became even closer.

She was the last one he would see when he left town, and the first one he visited when he returned. Their bond of love and respect was not to be broken.

Fatima made what was to be the farewell pilgrimage with her father (pbuh). She wept when the verse was revealed, "This day I have perfected for you your religion and completed My favor upon you and have approved for you Islam as your religion." 5:3, as she knew that this meant his death was near. That year Jabriel (pbuh), instead of reviewing the Qur'an with the Prophet (pbuh) once, reviewed it twice, signaling the end of the time of revelation.

As the Prophet (pbuh) was passing away, he whispered something to Fatima and she wept, but then he whispered something else to her

Unearthing Hidden Jewels

and she smiled. When Aisha asked her about this, she told her that her father (pbuh) said he would meet his Lord soon, and so she wept, but then he (pbuh) said that she would be with him soon, and that is what made her smile. She died six months after her father (pbuh). Ali washed her body, and she was laid in her grave.

Goodness comes from goodness, and Fatima was one of the four best women of the world. May her joy be complete now.

~~~

From the characteristics of the companions was that they used to enjoin good and forbid evil, even if they were struggling to do good themselves. They knew that no soul could be good all the time, but the real work was recognizing this in themselves and then others, and reminding of good. One said, "If the sinners cannot rectify the disobedient, then, who after Mohammad (pbuh) can do this?"

Sufyaan ath-Thawri (ra) was asked, "Should a person order the good if he knows that the other person will reject it?" He replied, "Yes, so that he is forgiven in the sight of Allah for doing his duty."

Bringing It Forward to Today

What can we say about this sweet flower, this precious dawn in the life of our Prophet (pbuh)? Her commitment to her father is something to be admired and emulated. We cannot lose the respect for our parents, as they are our connection to the past, and our lessons for the future. Once that line is severed, we give up who we are, and become a sliver of dust, adhering to anything we come close to, and being picked up again and again by any passing wind. Our roots must go deep.

Commitment

Did You Know?

There was a famous queen in Yemen in the 1300s called Al Udar al Karima. Her son was the ruler of Yemen, which was a caliphate of Egypt at the time of his rule. He needed to go to war to protect Egypt, and so put his mother in charge of the country.

This woman of piety, goodness, and extreme intelligence made more changes in her fourteen months of rule than her son did the whole time he was in charge.

She established justice, charity, security, and religious scholarship.

She would secretly go from home to home to see if anything was needed, and when she found a need, she was very generous.

She built two exceptional schools around the city of Zabiid, and many mosques were built, staffed, and maintained under her care. She had the utmost of respect for any pious man who worked in her mosques, and afforded them great honor in their positions.

Her generosity and patience became legendary in her time, and she will be remembered as the "true daughter of Balqis", another famous ruler of Yemen mentioned in the Qur'an.

Unearthing Hidden Jewels

GENEROSITY–A RICH AND LILTING ENDOWMENT

"And establish prayer and give zakah, and whatever good you put forward for yourselves – you will find it with Allah. Indeed, Allah is the All-Seeing of what you do." {The Qur'an, 2:110}

A songbird moves through to delight all around it, giving freely of its proclamation of good and all that is rapturous of the moment. These dainty, neatly packaged "poets of the sky" dart about doing their daily tasks, spreading the melody of one who is confident in the message they bring. Their unique trill rises about the din of humanity as they ride the soft currents aloft. They sweeten the air, not allowing the tumultuous hoards below to tug at the harmony of the heavens and the earth gifted to those who reside between the two.

This golden-throated companion delighted even the Prophet (pbuh) with his recitation of the Qur'an...

ABDULLAH BIN MAS'UD

Quote: *"A generous heart, kind speech, and a life of service and compassion are things which renew humanity."* – Anonymous

Abdullah bin Mas'ud was a young boy, not yet to the age of puberty, and was herding the sheep of one of the Quraish. He would take the flock everyday up to the mountain passes around Makkah, which took him far away from the society around him. He had heard of the Prophet (pbuh), but didn't pay much mind to it all.

One day as he was tending his sheep, two men appeared over a hill and came walking towards him. They looked quite worn out, and as they came closer, they greeted him warmly.

Generosity

One of them said, "Hey, young boy. Can you milk this ewe for us so that we may refresh ourselves?"

"I cannot," the boy answered, "the sheep are not mine. They are only under my care and trust."

Rather than being angry, the two men seemed pleased.

One of them said, "Show us an ewe which has not yet had a lamb, and does not produce milk." The young boy pointed to one, and the man went to her, put his arm around her neck, and passed his hand over her udder while speaking the name of Allah. Soon, the udder swelled with milk, and the other man found a concave stone, and this was filled and each one drank his fill of milk from it.

When they were done, the man again passed his hand over the udder and said, "Shrink," and the ewe returned to its natural state.

The boy looked at the man and said, "Teach me these words." The man smiled and said, "You already know them."

Abdullah became very fond of this man and his companion who had taken shelter in the hills from the persecution going on in Makkah. Soon the boy converted and offered himself to the Prophet (pbuh) as a servant. He eventually became so trusted that he went traveling with the Prophet (pbuh), he spent time in his home, he would awaken him, screen him when he bathed, fetch his sandals when he wanted to go out, and remove them when he came in. He carried his staff and *miswak*, and slept in a room next to the blessed Prophet (pbuh).

The Prophet (pbuh) kept nothing hidden from this quiet boy until he became known as "the keeper of the Prophet's (pbuh) secrets".

Unearthing Hidden Jewels

As the boy grew, he took on the attributes and virtues of the Prophet (pbuh), so much so that people said he was more similar to him than anyone else. Ibn Mas'ud was the most knowledgeable of the Qur'an and its meaning, as well as the Divine Law. Many of the surahs were recited directly to him right after they were revealed. One time, the Prophet (pbuh) asked Ibn Mas'ud to recite to him. Ibn Mas'ud replied, "Should I recite to you, and you are the one the Qur'an was revealed on?" The Prophet (pbuh) said, "Yes, but I love to hear it from other than me." So, Ibn Mas'ud started reciting surat an-Nisa, but when he reached the words of Allah, *"So how will it be when We bring from every nation a witness and we bring you against these people as a witness?"* (Surah 4:41), The Prophet (pbuh) told him, "That's enough," as he (pbuh) was overcome with tears.

Ibn Mas'ud was slight and his legs were extremely thin. One day, the Prophet (pbuh) asked him to climb a tree to retrieve something for him, and when the companions saw the size of his legs, they laughed. The Prophet (pbuh) turned to them and said, "Why do you laugh? One of his legs will weigh more than the mountain of Uhud on the Day of Judgment!"

Umar (ra) told a story of he and Abu Bakr sitting with the Prophet (pbuh) and discussing some concerns of the community, when the Prophet (pbuh) suddenly got up and went out the door. They followed him until all three came upon a man in the masjid reciting Qur'an. They could not see who he was because of the darkness, but then the Prophet (pbuh) said, "If any one of you wishes to recite the Qur'an as purely as it was first revealed, let him recite it as Ibn Mas'ud does."

Ibn Mas'ud himself said that there was not a single verse in the Qur'an that he didn't know when and where it was revealed, and under what circumstances. He added, though, that if he knew of someone with more knowledge, he would travel to him to learn from him.

Son of Umm 'abd, as the Prophet (pbuh) affectionately called him, was a brave and strong fighter in the way of Allah, and showed this by being the second person, after the Prophet (pbuh), to recite the Qur'an publicly. This was early on, when the Muslims were few in number, and heavily persecuted. They were discussing that the people of Quraish had not yet heard the Qur'an, and Ibn Mas'ud said, "I will recite it to them!"

Of course, the companions were fearful that he would be hurt or even killed, but he insisted. He went to the Kabah and began, and was struck on the face over and over, but took it as long as he could, and then went back to the companions, bloodied, but strong in his commitment to Islam.

When the Prophet (pbuh) died, the only consolation for Ibn Mas'ud was that he knew that the Prophet (pbuh) was pleased with him when he stated, "Hold tight to the covenant of the son of Umm Abd." He (pbuh) also said, "I am content for my people with what the son of Umm Abd is content with, and I dislike for my people with what the son of Umm Abd dislikes."

There is a wonderful story of Umar and his caravan traveling in the darkness of night, and coming across another caravan, and Umar asked many questions trying to ascertain who they were. Every single one of his questions about Islam and the Qur'an were answered perfectly, and that is how he found out that Ibn Mas'ud was traveling with them. Umar was so impressed with Ibn Mas'ud's humility, piety, and knowledge of the Qur'an that he sent him all the way to Koofah in Iraq to be minister there.

Ibn Mas'ud lived until the time of Uthman, and died reciting the Book he so loved.

Just before his death a man came to him and said he had seen him in a dream. The man said, "The Prophet (pbuh) was on the mimbar and you were below him. He (pbuh) spoke to you and said, "Oh, Ibn Mas'ud, come to me. You are so lonely without me!" Ibn Mas'ud made the man swear by Allah that this was true. This is how he knew that death was near.

He was remembered by the companions when they had a memory about the Prophet (pbuh). His sweet recitation of the Qur'an would resound in their ears and nourish their hearts as if they were hearing it for the first time.

May Allah allow him to sing with the green birds of Paradise…

~~~

From the characteristics of the Companions was that they would pardon and overlook those who would cause them harm. They followed in the footsteps of our Prophet (pbuh) who never retaliated on his own behalf, but did so only when the boundaries of Allah were crossed.

They believed, and rightly so, that anyone who followed this was closer to the mercy of the Most Merciful. Surah Maidah 5:13 says, *"Pardon them and overlook, Allah loves those who do good."*

Qataadah was asked, "Which person has the highest standing with Allah?" and he quickly replied, "The one most abundant in his pardon!"

Bringing it Forward to Today

We seem to forget that we were all created with a special purpose in mind by our Creator. What is that one trait, characteristic, talent, desire, or goal that makes you different than anyone else? We should try to pinpoint this and nurture it, and then bring it forward to the people for the good effect it can have on society. Come on, we all have something inside of us that is waiting to be deepened and brought out at just the right time for maximum benefit. We are nobler than the angels because we have free will, and therefore getting through the obstacles has more worth to Allah. Push through, and Allah will reward accordingly. The one who works slowly will not be prevented from his share, and the one who works eagerly will not get more than is decreed for them of worldly pursuits.

Did You Know?

Zheng He, a famous Chinese explorer, was actually born in Central Asia as a Muslim. He was captured by the Chinese army who had invaded and conquered the Mongols. They took him back to China, and ritually castrated him, but he grew to be a towering genius with amazing leadership abilities. He became a personal bodyguard for Zhu Di, who, with the help of Zheng He, seized imperial power.

Unearthing Hidden Jewels

Zheng He was made Admiral of the Chinese navy and made seven epic journeys to over 30 countries, a full 70 years before Columbus.

His fleet was like a floating metropolis, with ships over 400 feet long and 180 feet wide. If you were to compare Columbus's ship, the 'Nina', at only 75 feet, it pales in comparison.

His fleet included 317 ships with 27,800 crew members to sail them. He carried zebras, oryx, and ostriches on board, and used otters working in pairs to herd fish into nets to feed his hungry crew.

The Eternal Harvest

"Indeed, the men who practice charity and the women who practice charity and they who have loaned Allah a goodly loan - it will be multiplied for them, and they will have a noble reward."
{The Qur'an, 57:18}

Once there was a twisted and knarly vine, born in darkness, growing and creeping over anything it touched. It found joy in its dark ways, making sure its tendrils blotted out any goodness in its path.

One day it realized it carried the beginnings of a blossom, a seed of its sunless soul, a twilight fruit of shadowy intention. The noxious vine watched proudly as this seed began its journey through the dimly-lit shaft. The seedling twisted and turned, thinking it was part of this dastardly tunnel, but when it finally felt the rush of air, the oppressive shaft fell away, bathing the seed in a cleansing light. It gave a final push to freedom, vibrant with goodness and hardly recognizable to its progenitor. The living is drawn from the dead…

This exquisite companion from rather dubious roots was a giving soul shrouded by lineage.

'Akrimah bin Abu Jahl

Quote: *"Overlook and forgive the weakness of generous people, because if they fall down, Allah (SWT) gives his hand in their hands and helps them..."* – Ali ibn Abu Talib

'Akrimah was in his late twenties when Mohammad (pbuh) proclaimed the message of Islam. He was of the tribe of Quraish, of noble rank, wealth, and power. He watched as his peers accepted Islam, but he was his father's son, and diametrically opposed to the message, as was his father, Abu Jahl. His father made him to be a staunch opponent of the Muslims, and he became one of the Prophet's (pbuh) worst enemies. He insulted, persecuted and harassed anyone who accepted the call.

In the battle of Badr, he and his father fought, but did not attain victory, and his father was killed, and in the hasty retreat 'Akrimah was not able to retrieve his father's body. His hatred of the Muslims and their cause, after this, knew no bounds. Now, for him, it was revenge, which can be more intense than just opposition. He and his friends who had lost loved ones in Badr went around stirring up trouble and hostility, and then had their chance at the battle of Uhud. He and Khalid ibn Walid, who was not Muslim yet, turned the tide for the pagans on the battlefield, and they had bragging rights for a while, but then came the Battle of the Trench. They tried to bridge the trench, but failed, and had to run to save themselves from destruction.

When the Prophet (pbuh) and his followers re-entered Makkah, they said that they would not fight anyone who did not fight them. The tribal leaders wanted to simply open the gates without opposition, as the numbers against them were huge, but 'Akrimah and his band went against their leaders and said they would fight them. Khalid ibn Walid, now a Muslim, defeated this renegade group easily, and those who were not killed in the skirmish ran away.

'Akrimah wasn't sure what to do next. He was an outcast in his own city, and although the Prophet (pbuh) had declared amnesty for most of the Quraish, 'Akrimah was not one of those pardoned. He headed for Yemen, as his wife headed for the home of the Prophet (pbuh) to declare Islam and her loyalty to him. She asked the Prophet (pbuh) to grant her husband security, which he did, and she left immediately to find her husband to tell him the good news. She hooked up with some Bedouins, and traveled until she reached the Red Sea. 'Akrimah had boarded a ship, and had his own adventure. The seas became deadly and the people on board wanted to have fewer people on the ship to make it easier to survive. 'Akrimah prayed at that moment and said, "Oh, Allah, if you let me live, I will go back and put my hand in the hand of your Messenger." He did come back to port safely, and was surprised to find his wife waiting for him there. She came up to him and told him that she had come from the most pious, and he had guaranteed his safety. She had to talk for a long time until he was convinced that he would be safe. They started back to Makkah together, and she resisted any contact with him because, she said, "I am a Muslim, and you are a pagan!" 'Akrimah saw how seriously she took her Islam, and honored that.

As they approached Makkah, the Prophet (pbuh) told those around him, "'Akrimah ibn Abu Jahl will come to you as a believer, so do not curse his father, for cursing the dead offends the living, but does not affect the dead."

Soon the two arrived, and in his joy, the Prophet (pbuh) jumped up and forgot to cover himself with his cloak. When he had greeted them, and sat down again 'Akrimah approached him, asking him if he was truly safe from any repercussions.

The Prophet (pbuh) answered in the affirmative.

"Then, what are you calling me to?" 'Akrimah asked.

The Prophet (pbuh) then enumerated the pillars and beliefs, and 'Akrimah agreed that these were the truth, and what was ordered of him was righteousness. He had always known Muhammad (pbuh) to be the truthful, and the charitable one. 'Akrimah, as a child, was blessed by the *du'a* of the Prophet (pbuh) at Ta'if when the angel came and asked if the Prophet (pbuh) wanted to destroy those who had rejected him. He (pbuh) said, "No, I pray that their offspring might worship Allah." All these years later 'Akrimah was there extending his hand and becoming Muslim. He asked for forgiveness for his aggression against the Muslims, and the Prophet (pbuh) asked Allah for his forgiveness. With this, the face of 'Akrimah lit up, and he said, "I swear by Allah, that as for me, I will spend for the sake of Allah twice the money which I spent to keep people from believing in Allah. I will spend, as a mujahid for the sake of Allah, twice the energy I spent doing battle to keep people from Islam." He had to endure insults in the beginning and they became so bad that he went back and complained to the Prophet (pbuh). The Prophet (pbuh) went out to the people and said, "Men are like different metals and the best of you in Islam do not insult a Muslim with a disbeliever."

After this, 'Akrimah was a fierce warrior, a devout worshipper, and a constant reciter of Qur'an. He would hold the book to his face, weeping and saying, "The words of my Lord, the words of my Lord…"

He fought in every battle, and at the battle of Yarmuk, when it appeared that the Muslims would be defeated, 'Akrimah jumped off his horse and broke the holder for his sword, intending to fight to the death. Khalid tried to stop him, but 'Akrimah pointed out how much he needed to catch up on good deeds after tormenting the Muslims for so many years.

He turned to the group of soldiers and asked, "Who will fight to the death with me?"

He had four hundred takers, and they fought so fiercely that the battle was won, but not without tremendous loss to the Muslims, as he and two of his brave companions lay dying on the battlefield. These three valiant companions faced their death with dignity, refusing the water offered to each other until they saw that the other two had quenched their thirst. This did not happen, as they all met the Highest Companion before any of them took a sip. May Allah grant 'Akrimah and his fellow warriors the taste of Salsabil for eternity, ameen.

~~~

From the characteristics of the companions was that they gave bounteous charity day and night, in secret and openly. The poor amongst them at least spared the people their harm, and bore the harm of others as charity.

Abdul-Azeez ibn Umar (ra) said, "Salat will get you down half the road, fasting lets you reach the door of the King, and charity allows you to enter into the King's company."

Their manners were that they would not suspect beggars, and would always think that these poor begged from dire need.

Sufyan ath-Thawri (ra), used to run to his door, joyful when he

Unearthing Hidden Jewels

saw someone in need, saying, "Welcome to the one who has come to wash my sins."

Bringing it Forward to Today

There are so many lessons to be gleaned from this companion. First, don't judge what you see on the outside. Allah Almighty looks at the hearts, and only He can truly see them for what they are. We can only see the skin, eyes, facial expressions, and we can hear their words. It's not always enough to go on, and so we really need to leave the judgment to Al-Adl, the Just, and go by outward appearances.

Secondly, this companion allowed Islam to wash him of all his previous thoughts and actions, cleanse him of all he had built up about Islam and Muslims. We could use Islam in the same way. Allow it to enter our hearts and minds and wash away the pent-up feelings we harbor for our fellow human beings. Submit in the dark of the night, and you will find peace. Isn't this what Islam means?

Did You Know?

The first real advance in "cracking codes" came in the 800s by a Muslim named Al-Kindi. He was appointed by several Abbasid Caliphs to oversee the translation of Greek scientific and philosophical papers into Arabic, and this allowed him to move forward in many fields of study. One such field was Mathematics.

As the "mail carrier" in the 9th century was a pigeon, messages needed to have a method of being made confidential, and so coding was used. Cairo at the time had 1,900 carrier pigeons in its 'mail central'.

Al-Kindi began studying in depth the Arabic Qur'an, and he noticed that certain letters were used more frequently than others. He then used this information to compile a code-breaking method he called "frequency analysis". Many people thought that substitution ciphers were unbreakable before this.

This method was used effectively all the way up to World War II.

His book, *Treatise on Deciphering Cryptographic Messages* opened the way for modern cryptology, and the path for cultures other than his own to break and encode messages.

The Selfless Outpouring

"[O Muhammad], tell My servants who have believed to establish prayer and spend from what We have provided them, secretly and publicly, before a Day comes in which there will be no exchange, nor any friendships." {The Qur'an, 14:31}

Where is the relief when the mighty and resplendent ocean swells to its capacity and beyond? It thrusts itself down the spider-like tributaries, but even these cannot hold its overflowing bounty. When this torrent finally reaches the edge of the earth, it spills over, crashing and tumbling, showering its profuse abundance on the land below. This lavish magnanimity brings blessings to all it caresses.

So too, the charity of this companion blessed all that it touched. ..

Abdurrahman bin Auf

Quote: *"We make a living by what we get; we make a life by what we give."* – Anonymous

Abdurrahman bin Auf was one of the first eight who accepted Islam and one of the ten promised Paradise. He was persecuted along with the others brave enough to declare the truth, and made the trip to Abyssinia twice, and also later, made the hijra to Madina. There he was paired up in brotherhood with Sa'd ibn AlRabi'. Sa'd said to him, "I am the richest of the Ansar. Let me grant you one half of my wealth." Abdurrahman thanked him warmly and said, "I am not in need of all of this. Show me to the market!"

This prodigious companion was so talented at trade that even his wealth had wealth. He also owned a farm so vast that it took twenty camels to irrigate his fields. One of his trade caravans included seven hundred camels loaded with wheat, flour, and various foodstuffs. One of these multitudinous caravans caught the eye and ear of Aisha (ra), and she narrated a *hadith* about how wealth often degrades a person, and when Abdurrahman heard this, he ran to her and swore that he had given the whole caravan, camels and all, away in the sake of Allah.

He didn't stop there; he gave away fully half of his wealth in the cause of Islam. He then offered another forty thousand dinars, and at a later call for help in jihad, he offered five hundred horses, and five hundred camels.

None could compete with him in the setting free of slaves, as he set thirty slaves free in a single day. He sold some land for forty thousand dinars, and gave that away in charity. After all this, he still worried that his wealth would prove to be harmful in the hereafter, so he was advised by Umm Salamah to, "Spend as much as you can in the way of Allah!"

Whenever he would be served good food, he would remember the Day of Judgment and begin to weep, remembering the days when the companions (ra) couldn't get enough to eat. He would most times end up refusing the meal.

He readily gave up his family name and when he did his hijrah to Madina, the wealth he accrued did not make him weak, soft, or cowardly. He fought in the front lines at the Battle of Badr and fought so bravely in the Battle of Uhud that he was wounded twenty times. At one point in the heat of the battle, The Prophet (pbuh) asked where he was. Al Harith said Abdurrahman was fighting a group of disbelievers at the foot of Uhud. The Prophet (pbuh) then told Al Harith, "The angels are beside him, fighting!" His foot was injured very badly, and it never did heal, making him limp for the rest of his life on earth. During the Battle of Tabouk, the Prophet (pbuh) had to leave on business for a while. Those present asked Abdurrahman to lead the prayer. When the Prophet (pbuh) returned, he got into the line of prayer behind Adurrahman, and after he completed his prayer he said, "No prophet has passed away until he has prayed behind a good man of his nation."

When this intelligent, gentle man was sent to the tribe of Kalb, and was told to give them dawah, his truthful manner allowed him to bring in the whole village in three days time. He had been instructed to marry the daughter of the chief of the tribe, which he did.

His counsel was so valued that after the death of the Prophet (pbuh), his advice was sought for the successor, and they were able to take his suggestions and settle the matter quickly. He became a valued advisor to Abu Bakr (ra), and was nominated for third caliph, but he withdrew his name and recommended Uthman instead.

Umm Salamah said she heard the Prophet (pbuh) say, "The one who treats you with passion and tenderness after my death is honest and righteous. Oh, Allah, give Abdurrahman a drink from Salsabil in Paradise."

He died around the age of seventy five, but to sum up his character, he was entrusted with the safety and took responsibility for the wives of the Prophet (pbuh), second only to the Prophet himself. What more can be said about the consistent nature of this generous, caring man.

His son, Talha, said his father lent one third of his wealth, relieved debt with another third, and preserved relationships with the final third.

May Allah be generous with this man of giving…

~~~

From the characteristics of the companions was their absolute obedience to the saying of the Prophet (pbuh), "Whoever believes in Allah and the Last Day, then he should be generous towards his guest!"

They would serve the guests themselves, if possible, and would never think that they had sufficiently fed them.

They believed that the reward of a guest was entertainment for a day and night with high-quality food, then three days with ordinary food, and anything after that was charity.

Anas ibn Malik (ra) used to say that the zakat of one's home was to keep a room there for guests. The companions used to condemn anyone who did not honor his visitors.

Bringing it Forward to Today

The lesson here is the unbounded fear of Allah in all matters. Not just fear, but actually putting all that He commanded into full practice in the life. Sometimes you can find someone with one or two traits that are desirable, but here was a man, a leader, who had so many. Another lesson to grasp is that this companion was a gateway for Allah's blessings, and that gate was always swung wide open. The word conduit comes to mind, and that is something that only one who fears Allah, and nothing of this world can be. Do we have even an ounce of this fear, this fear that transforms, this fear that makes us know that giving is getting? May we learn from this giving soul how to truly pour forth…

Unearthing Hidden Jewels

Did You Know?

The Muslim Geographer, Al-Idrisi, made a silver globe for King Roger II of Sicily (1097-1154), on a 400 kilogram round of silver. On this was recorded the seven continents, known trade routes, lakes, rivers, major cities, plains, and mountains. All were recorded with proper distance, length, and height.

He spent fifteen years making maps to add to the atlas for this King.

Very early on, Muslims were inspired by Greek and Persian manuscripts, and took things a step further. Al-Idrisi, to create the first world atlas, used the accurate measurements of the earth's surface already calculated by 9th century Muslim Astronomers, and several complete maps of the world, one of which was done in 1073 by a Turkish Geographer. This was 100 years before the travels of Marco Polo.

Christopher Columbus used a map of Al-Idrisi's, along with other Muslim Geographers on his journey to "discover" America.

The Heart that Mends

"Who spend in the cause of Allah during ease and hardship, and who restrain anger, and who pardon the people – and Allah loves the doers of good." {The Qur'an, 3:134}

When does the healer become the healed? When they are assisting the divine work of healing, they know that all factors working inside the wound are Allah's. All factors outside the wound are a matter of their will, caring, accrued knowledge, and drive.

When does the healer become the healed? When they enhance the natural course of healing by helping stop the blood flow, by applying something to close and protect, a cooling salve to bring in the fauna of herbal regeneration on a temporary binding skin. They are mimicking nature, with its innate instinct to make right what is wrong. By becoming a fluid part of any healing process, the healer feels she is fulfilling her function, bridging the gap between a natural process that might come too late to save the precious life force. With a healthy, healed patient who goes on to do much good, she is Allah's tool, like the cells that secrete, connect, and ultimately step out of the way of the Master Healer.

This caring female companion had a generosity of spirit…

Rufaidah Aslamiyyah

Quote: *"No one is useless in this world who lightens the burdens of it for anyone else."* – Charles Dickens

Rufaidah bint Saad al Aslamiyyah was an Ansari woman. Her father, Saad, was a physician, and she gained critically important knowledge under his tutelage. She then devoted herself to learning all she could about nursing, surgery, medicines, and how to best care for those around her. She used her skills to develop the first "mobile care units" which allowed her to go around to teach hygiene and prepare patients for surgery.

She was one of the first to embrace Islam in Madina, and she became an expert in the field of medicine for her time. She kept a tent ready for first aid and surgery at all times.

She and the nurses she trained from the female companions requested of the Prophet (pbuh) that they be allowed to go to battle with the men and treat the wounded. When they treated other than family, they only touched the affected part, and therefore maintained the proper decorum, even in the most chaotic of places. The Prophet (pbuh) allowed this, and was so impressed with their skills that he gave Rufaidah a part of the booties of war, just as he did the soldiers.

During the Battle of the Trench, she had a small clinic set up to treat the wounded, and all were referred to her for her expertise in healing.

She is honored by name in a sahih hadeeth by Bukhari in his book, "Al-Adab Al-Mufrad" as the one who treated the sick and wounded.

Some famous female companions who trained under her and went to battle with her were: Umm Ammara, Aminah, Umm Ayman, Safiyat, Umm Sulaim, and Hind, wife of Abu Sufyan.

Rufaiyah was known for her kindness, empathetic ways, and as an excellent organizer. During times of peace, she treated the sick, and did social work, helping the poor and orphans, training them for the general skills of life, and all that they might need.

Florence Nightingale has been touted for years as the first nurse in history, but Rufaidah bint Sa'ad was many centuries before her, and a source of pride for this *Ummah*.

May Allah heal her wounds with the salve of Jannah, ameen.

~~~

From the characteristics of the companions was their having such tender hearts that they would weep out of knowing the deficiencies they had in their devotion to Allah.

Ali (ra) said he had seen the companions before, but now he saw no one like them. He spoke of how they would arise in the morning dusty, pale, and with disheveled hair from spending the night in prostration. He said, "By Allah, it is as if I am now with people who have slept forgetful!"

Ka'b al-Ahbar (ra) said, "I prefer to weep out of the fear of Allah with only one teardrop than to spend a mountain of gold with an ungracious heart."

Bringing it Forward to Today

How often do we forget the unsung heroes? They are the ones who stay behind the lines and keep those same lines supplied with what we need. How quickly would the lines falter without this support? So when we see a famous Imam, let's remember who got him there; a good and righteous mother and father, supporting and helping him through his studies. When we see a brave soldier, let's remember who fed him, clothed him, taught him, and kept him safe. We need to honor those who do jobs no one else wants to do, but are so important to our cleanliness and well-being where we live, work, and study. Look around. These are true heroes, without whom we'd be without our "backbone". Dig deep and give gratitude where it is due.

Unearthing Hidden Jewels

Did You Know?

One of the first major hospitals in the Muslim world was built in Cairo, Egypt between 872 and 874 as a dispensary on the end of the grand Tulun Mosque. It was equipped with medicines and attendants, and had over one-hundred thousand books on the various branches of medicine, whereas the largest library in Europe at the time was at the University of Paris, with only four hundred books to refer to.

Harun Rashid built a center for medicine earlier than that, around 805, and this was called a bimaristan or asylum of the sick. These efforts at establishing healing for all became the "cradle of Islamic Medicine" These places of healing had a three-fold purpose: they spawned mobile dispensaries, first aid centers, and permanent hospitals.

Within decades, over thirty-four of these hospitals had sprung up around the Muslim world, with an additional fifty of them in Cordoba, Spain.

Care was free and available to all.

In one of these hospitals, a patient was called "cured" when he or she could ingest bread and a whole roasted bird in one sitting.

OBEDIENCE – THE AMENABLE SOUL

"O you who have believed, obey Allah and obey the Messenger and those in authority among you." {The Qur'an, 4:59}

Is not obedience courage? Does it not take courage when, as a physician in a war zone, you are called to the bedside of a critically wounded young man. You approach the stretcher and this precious, waning soul is your own son. Does it not take courage to say, "To Allah we belong and to Him we will return," and gently close the eyes after the soul has been lovingly lifted from a body no longer able to sustain it? Is this not obedience to the One who has said, "Grieve for three days, and then leave him to Me. He is My affair now." Yes, this is the courage of obedience.

Is not obedience asceticism? When you are told to use this lifetime only to get to Jannah, and leave the rest, and you do this at every twist and turn of life. Is this not obedience? It is the subtle acquiescence of obedience, as you are faced with the pull of the glitter of frivolity wherever you look. Yes, this is the contented and simple asceticism of obedience.

This exemplary companion had both of these endearing qualities, and much more…

ABDULLAH BIN JAHSH

Quote: *"In the heart there is an emptiness that cannot be filled except with love for Allah and by turning to Him, and always remembering Him. If one is given the entire world and what is in it, still it will not fill this emptiness."* – Imam Ibn al-Qayyim

Unearthing Hidden Jewels

Abdullah bin Jahsh was the first cousin of the Prophet (pbuh), his mother being the sister of the Prophet's (pbuh) father. He was also a brother-in-law, as the Prophet (pbuh) was married to his sister, Zaynab.

He was one of the first to accept Islam, even before the word was allowed to be said in the open. He went to Abyssinia, and was the second Muslim to leave on hijrah to Madina. Madina was different for him, though, as he brought with him his entire family, leaving behind all that he and his kin owned. When Abu Jahl went to the "ghost town" where the Muslims used to live, he saw the opulent home Abdullah had left, and grabbed it for his own.

Abdullah was upset over this, and went to complain to the Prophet, and the Prophet (pbuh) said to him, "Are you not content, Abdullah, that Allah shall provide for you a better home in Paradise, in place of the one you left for His sake?"

This promise from his prophet (pbuh) became much dearer to him than anything of this world from then on. When he was asked to go on a military excursion with seven others, and was made the first commander of the believers on this mission, he wanted to obey without delay. They were given a letter, only to be opened after two days of travel, and in it was written, "When you read this letter, you must travel until you reach Nakhlah, between Ta'if and Makkah. There you must observe the movements of the Quraish, and bring us news of them."

Abdullah then informed his companions that they did not have to continue with him, and had the choice to turn back at that point. The group answered as one that they "would accompany him

Obedience

to wherever the Prophet of Allah (pbuh) commands."

They began their scouting, but in the midst of this, they saw a caravan with four men of the Quraish. As this was the last day of a sacred month, they hesitated to attack, but if they waited until the day was over, these men would be in the sanctified boundary of Makkah, and the men knew they would not violate this. They finally agreed to attack right then, and killed one, took two of the men prisoner, and the fourth one got away. They headed back to Madina with the caravan and prisoners in tow.

When they arrived home, the Prophet (pbuh) severely condemned what they did saying, "By Allah, I did not command you to fight, but to observe." The Prophet (pbuh) ordered the prisoners detained and no one was to touch the contents of the caravan.

Abdullah and his seven companions were grieved so badly, as they thought they had disobeyed their Prophet (pbuh). How could Allah be pleased with them if they had done that? The Muslims around them made remarks about them being in disobedience to the Prophet (pbuh), and this made them feel even worse. Just when they thought they could not feel any worse, they heard that the Quraish were using this as a way to discredit the Prophet (pbuh) and his mission, and they were depressed beyond any description. It was at this most dejected moment that a Muslim came to them and told them that Allah had revealed a verse that vindicated them, *"They ask you about fighting in the sacred month. Say, 'fighting at that time is a grave offence, but graver is it in the sight of Allah to prevent access to the path of Allah, to deny Him, to prevent access to the sacred mosque and drive out its members. Tumult and oppression are worse than slaughter.'"* (2:217) At this revelation, the Prophet (pbuh) then embraced them and showed his approval.

This was significant because it was the first military action and the first booty of war taken. The one who died was the first pagan to die in battle, and the captives were the first taken under the banner of La ilaha illallah.

Abdullah then fought bravely in the battle of Badr and when it came to the battle of Uhud, he made a supplication to Allah which said, "Oh, Allah, send me a powerful warrior that I may do battle with him, and let him overcome me and cut off my nose and ear. I wish this so that when I meet You, You can ask me why I have my nose and ear cut off, and I can answer that I did it in Your sake, and You shall say that I have spoken the truth."

At the end of the battle, Abdullah bin Jahsh was killed, and his nose and ear were tied by a thread and hanging from a tree. He died as a martyr, just as his uncle, Hamza, did and the Prophet (pbuh), wetting the ground with his tears, buried Abdullah with his beloved uncle in the same grave. May the earth caress them both gently, these men who gave the ultimate sacrifice.

~~~

From the characteristics of the companions was their constant evaluation of the level of their piety, never claiming to be pious at all. The Prophet (pbuh) said that "piety is here" and he pointed to his chest, and the companions looked to their hearts to make sure they were acting according to Islam in every way.

Umar ibn Abdul Azeez (ra) used to say that the peak of piety is when someone can put all his thoughts and desires that are in his heart on a plate and carry it around the market, not being ashamed of anything there.

Abu Darda (ra) said, "The completion of Taqwa is to fear your Lord even over something as small as the weight of an atom.

Sufyaan ath-Thawri (ra) said, "We met a people who loved it when you said to them "Fear Allah!" Today you find that people only become annoyed at this."

BRINGING IT FORWARD TO TODAY

Whom do we obey? Is it our parents, our friends, our husbands, our wives, some sports star or singer, someone in a popular magazine that we give our allegiance to? Does this feel right? Shouldn't it be the One who created us, and knows what is best for us, and the one He sent to be our best example? Let's look at our lives and see who we have chosen to be our leader and then stop and take a good look at them. Will obedience to them get us to the Paradise, our ultimate goal? Only you can decide, and all hope is that you make the right choice.

Did You Know?

The destruction of the House of Wisdom in Baghdad did not come at the hands of Genghis Khan, but his grandson, Hulagu. Hulagu's goal was to conquer Persia, Syria, and Egypt, and to destroy the Abbasid Caliph.

He was able to do this easily because the Abbasid Caliph had shrunk to only ruling Baghdad, and the Caliphate was more concerned with its gold and riches than anything else, Persia was disunited, and Salah al-Din controlled only parts of Iraq and Syria.

The only governorship able to stop the destructive force of the Mongols from overrunning Makkah and Medinah were the recently-throned Mamluks in Egypt.

In the early years, the House of Wisdom was the center of learning and discovery, bringing on the 'Golden Age of Islam', but by this time the center had moved to Muslim Spain, and the Abbasids were weak at the hands of the Mongol hoards. It only took two weeks to conquer Baghdad, and it is said that they killed between two-hundred thousand and one million people.

The Mongols destroyed mosques, hospitals, libraries, and palaces. The Tigris River ran black with the ink of years of Islamic knowledge.

Amazingly, when all seemed lost in the Muslim world, the conquerors, over the next few generations, came to Islam. This was the first time in history that the victors took on the religion of the conquered.

The Abiding Heart

"And whoever obeys Allah and the Messenger will be in the company of those whom Allah has blessed, the Prophets, the truthful, the martyrs and the righteous. How excellent are those as companions." {The Qur'an, 4:69}

A lotus flower, resilient and pure, is rooted in the depths of a murky darkness. The blossom, encased in an overlay so smooth that no dirt can mar its flawless virtue, rises out of the mire. This tender shoot has to resist the vacuumous pull of the shadowy, somber gloom threatening to pull it under. It knows it must grow tall, reaching for the light, holding to the hope of a promise of warmth and bounty.

When it grows to its full height, the protective sheath gives way and the petals, the color of freshly fallen snow on a mountain, unfold, opening their arms wide to the sky. They never look back, balancing on the shimmering, sunlit mantle above the marshy bottom. They are an inspiration to all who care to wonder at their journey from darkness to light.

This companion also grew straight and tall, just like his father, the upholder of the Abrahamic faith…

Said bin Zaid

Quote: *"It make no difference to me anymore whether I wake up to find something I love or something I hate, for I do not know what is good for me in what I love or what I hate."* – Umar Ibn al-Khattab (ra)

Said bin Zaid embraced Islam as soon as he heard the Prophet's (pbuh) message, and why should he have hesitated. His father, Zaid, followed the religion of Abraham long before the Prophethood of Muhammad (pbuh). Zaid lived in the time of ignorance, but knew in his heart, when he looked around, that something didn't feel right. He asked and searched until he got enough to base his life on, and condemned the idolatry around him. He would not worship the idols, he would not eat the meat the people slaughtered in their names, and he questioned everything around him, as it seemed to contradict the oneness he felt was Allah's alone. His son grew up seeing this, and when Said, as a young man, heard the message of the Prophet (pbuh), he immediately became a Muslim, as did his obedient wife. The trouble was that his wife was the sister of the most ardent and powerful opponent of Islam, Umar ibn Al-Khattab. The tolerance of pagan family members to one of their own becoming Muslim was almost nil, so here is how the story of Umar's conversion unfolds:

The pagans of Makkah had reached such a frustration level that they sent Umar one day to kill the Prophet (pbuh), and Umar made ready his sword and left his home to do what he thought was the most important of services for his people. He was a formidable man, with great strength, and his stride was quick that day. On the road, he ran into someone he knew who asked where he was going with such purpose on his face. "I'm going to kill Muhammad!" was his quick reply.

"You better look to your own house before that, as your sister and her husband have embraced Islam!" this passerby taunted him.

Umar became very angry then, and headed to his brother-in-law's

Obedience

house in a rage. He began to beat Said, and when his sister tried to come between them, he began to beat her. She called out to him, "Oh Umar, you may take our lives, but you cannot take Islam out of our hearts. If you do not follow the truth, your Creator will take revenge on you!"

Umar stopped then and stood there with his mouth open. His sister's words hit him deeply, and he became calm. "Read to me, then, what you were reciting when I came to you," was his answer.

Said began to recite the Qur'an, and the truth of it settled into Umar's heart, and he immediately left to find the Prophet (pbuh) for a different reason. He wanted to become Muslim!

Said, throughout his life, never did anything against the teaching of Allah, and His Messenger (pbuh). A historian once said, "Said always covered the Prophet (pbuh), keeping himself ahead and in front of him in battle, and always stood behind him in prayers."

He fought bravely in every battle, and was offered a Governorship, which he refused. Once, without his permission, he was made Governor of Damascus, and he immediately wrote a letter asking to be relieved of this so he could fight in jihad instead. His perfect submission to faith, fear of Allah, and services for the cause of Islam earned him the glad tidings of Paradise from his beloved Prophet (pbuh). At the age of seventy, he left this earth to reap his Eternal reward. Ah, what a loss for earth, and a gain for the Heavens!

~~~

From the characteristics of the companions was a deep fear of Allah in the beginning of an action, that it might involve them in something sinful and incur punishment. At the end of the action, they would be afraid they would be praised for it, and lose all the blessings of it. They would also constantly fear dying on some evil deed, which would make them very careful at all times.

Abu Turab an-Nakhshabi (ra) would say, "If a person resolves to leave sinning, Allah sends him reinforcements from all sides. Three indications of the blackness of the heart are: Not finding an escape from sinning, or a place in it for obedience, or a haven for a sermon that warns."

It was said that if the only quality of obedience was light on the face and radiance, love in the heart, strength in the limbs, and security of the soul, all these would have been good enough reasons to leave sin.

Bringing It Forward To Today

Zaid was the best model for parenting. He was outspoken about believing in other than the oneness of Allah, loved Allah throughout his life, and raised his son to recognize the truth when he heard it. Children do not do what you say, they do what you do. This alone should be fair warning for the best of behaviors in the home and outside. Now more than ever, good role models are precious and as good as gold. People don't mind working all day if the source of the spring is pure and good.

Did You Know?

As far back as 105 C.E., papermaking began in China. They managed to keep it a secret for over 500 years, making woodblock prints as far back as the 700s.

In 751, the T'ang army was defeated by the Ottomans, and Chinese prisoners excellent in papermaking were taken to Samarkand, and this secret was finally shared with the Muslims.

The first papermaking mill was built in Baghdad in 793 C.E.

Muslim papermakers used newly-invented 'trip hammers' to beat linen rags and tree roots for use as pulp in the mills.

Better paper meant more books, and more books meant easier spreading of knowledge.

Pens started out being made of reeds, but in 953 the Sultan of Egypt asked for a pen that didn't leak, and was given a version of our fountain pens used in modern times.

More than one million books per year are published today. You are holding one of them!

THE SOUL THAT HEEDS

"O you, who have believed, respond to Allah and to the Messenger when he calls you to that which gives you life. And know that Allah intervenes between a man and his heart and that to Him you will be gathered." {The Qur'an, 8:24}

Let's say that you are part of a great and noble expedition. Your leader is focused and brave, filled to the brim with certainty of the destination. His vision for the journey's end is of exotic palaces of gold and silver, fruit trees bearing succulent harvest, and overwhelming peace and kindness contained within walls of embracing light and love.

The journey is long, though, and there are many side roads calling to you with sirens of promised satisfaction. You look down these shaded paths longingly, exhausted from the hot, dry travels. This wise leader sees the furtive looks and says, "No, be content with your meager provisions and stay straight on your path." Would you not be deferential to this advice of one whom you trust? This is the forbearance of obedience.

Your devotion to this leader would keep you on the path even when he is not with you. This is the commitment of obedience...

Our next companion was "master of the bow" and his arrow hit the mark in Islamic history.

SA'AD IBN ABI WAQQAS

Quote: *"Know that you will never truly love Allah until you love obeying Him."* – Hasan al-Basri

Obedience

Sa'ad Ibn Abi Waqqas, a maternal uncle of the Prophet (pbuh), was not yet twenty, but was training himself on the making of bow and arrow and archery as if awaiting a great battle. He hailed from a rich family and was considered serious and intelligent. Sharply aware of the paganism around him, he longed for the truth, so when Abu Bakr came and whispered in his ear one day of the revelation given to Muhammad (pbuh), he quickly got up and went to declare his Islam. You see, he was following a dream he previously had where he was surrounded by darkness and suddenly a bright moon came and lit his way. In his dream, he followed this lunar torch while in front of him were Abu Bakr, Ali, and Zayd.

The Prophet (pbuh) was pleased when Sa'ad came into the fold of Islam, because he felt enormous potential in his beautiful, young uncle. He knew what a rare and wonderful addition he would be to the small band of Believers.

Sa'ad mother, however, was not pleased. She and Sa'ad were very close, and she thought she could get him to give up this 'new religion' by threatening to go on a hunger strike. She told him she would not eat or drink until he came back to her beliefs. She stopped eating and drinking until she became very weak, but his answer was short and eloquent, "Dear mother, please don't do this because even if you had a thousand souls and each one departed one after another, I would not leave my religion." After this, his mother gave up her quest, and began to nourish herself.

Sa'ad was the first to shed blood in the conflict between believers and unbelievers. He had gone out of Makkah to pray with a group of

Unearthing Hidden Jewels

Muslims, so as not to rile up the pagans. When some of the disbelievers came upon them as they prayed, they started to taunt and abuse them. Sa'ad picked up a bone and hit one of them, drawing first blood. When they got back to Makkah and told the Prophet (pbuh), he advised them to be more patient and forbearing, as this was the command of their Lord.

Later, when the command shifted and the Muslims were asked to fight, Sa'ad immediately left for Badr with his much younger brother, Umayr, but unfortunately came back after the battle without him. Umayr had died a martyr on the battlefield that day. Sa'ad stood by the Prophet (pbuh) that day in the midst of the war and made a *dua*, "Oh, Allah, shake their feet with fear, terrify their hearts, and do with them what You wish." The Prophet (pbuh) stood behind him saying, "Oh, Allah, answer Sa'ad's prayer."

In the battle of Uhud, he was chosen as one of the lead archers, and came to the defense of the Prophet (pbuh) when some of the Muslims deserted their posts. He shot more than nine hundred arrows that day. Ali heard the Prophet (pbuh) say to Sa'ad as Sa'ad fought bravely to protect him, "Shoot Sa'ad, May my mother and father be your ransom." Ali had never before heard these words from the Prophet (pbuh) for anyone. The Prophet (pbuh) again prayed for Sa'ad, "Oh, Lord, direct his shooting and respond to his prayer." He was known after that as the one whose prayers were always answered.

One day the Prophet (pbuh) was sitting with some companions, and said, "The first one to enter this door is a man set for Paradise." When they turned, it was Sa'ad Ibn Abi Waqqas. A man followed him and asked him what he did to earn this, and Sa'ad said, "I do what we all do, except I never harbor a grudge against any Muslim."

Well known for his bravery and generosity. Umar sent him as the Commander in Chief against the Persians. When he sent him off to war, he gave him this reminder, "Oh Sa'ad, there is no connection between Allah and anyone except obedience to Him. Consider how the Messenger of Allah used to act with the Muslims, and act accordingly." Things looked dire on the battlefield as the Muslims were outnumbered, and were up against the might of the Persian Elephant Corps. Their only break came when Allah sent a storm to rip the tent up and off their leader and several Muslims headed straight for the Persian Commander. Rustum was killed and the Persian army became scattered and confused. Victory, after many devastating losses to the unbelievers, finally came to the Muslims. Chosroe's palace was eventually turned into a masjid, and Sa'ad sent all the priceless treasures to Umar, making Umar comment when he saw these riches before him, "Whoever sent this wealth is indeed trustworthy."

Umar sent Sa'ad to be Governor of Mada'in, and he and his army rode their horses across the waters of the Tigris as if they were walking on land. The Persian soldiers exclaimed when they saw this that, "We are not fighting men, we are fighting Jinn!" Sa'ad and Salman Farsi made many beautiful supplications to Allah as they crossed, and Salman commented that, "By Allah, the seas have surrendered to us just as the lands have." This event became known in history as "The Day of Water".

Later on, in the year 615, Sa'ad was deputed to go to China with three of his companions. They sailed by way of Abyssinia to China, and he made the long journey to these exotic lands two more times after that. The Emperor welcomed him warmly each time, and it is believed that Sa'ad had a mosque built there. The claim is that this could be one of the oldest mosques in the world. Islam flourished through trade in the years following these encounters.

Sa'ad Ibn Abi Waqqas was one of the ten companions promised Paradise in his lifetime. He was the last of these chosen ten to die and was buried in Madina. This noble companion was buried in a coarse, woolen robe he had worn in the Battle of Badr, and it had been his desire to meet his Lord in this. May Allah adorn him with layers of the softest silks.

~~~

From the characteristics of the companions was that they would continually advise one another, the elder not being offended by the youthfulness of the advisor. They would accept the advice, and even thank the one who gave it. The one advised would be grateful to the advisor for the rest of his life, as matters of the hereafter greatly outweigh the frivolous matters of this lifetime.

Taa'woos sent a letter to Makhool (ra) saying, "*Assalamulaikum*, my brother. Beware of regarding yourself as having a high standing in the sight of Allah, because of what you see of your actions. The one who thinks that about himself moves onto the Afterlife empty handed. The people may exalt you because of your good deeds, but that is so because your reward is hurriedly given to you in this world."

Obedience

BRINGING IT FORWARD TO TODAY

Subhan Allah, the last paragraph above, in the letter sent to Makhool is some of the best advice given. Do we allow others to exalt us with their flattery? We should always be afraid of the false flattery that makes others feel good about themselves by giving it. We need to look deeply into our hearts to see the truth, and weep to our Lord for our sins. He, alone, judges who we really are.

Did You Know?

Gunpowder was one of the four great inventions of the Chinese. The Mongols used it as they swept across the known world. What the Muslims did when they acquired this knowledge is they used it against the Mongols and the Crusaders.

A Muslim from 13th Century Syria named Hasan Al-Rammah experimented with the purifying of saltpeter until he was able to use it many different ways. He wrote a book called, The Book of Horsemanship and Ingenious War Devices with 107 recipes for the different levels of gunpowder. These were used in rockets, cannons, and fireworks.

Al-Rammah's book contained the first drawings of a torpedo made of iron with two rudders, a spear in front for lodging in the hull of the enemy ship, and carried a mix of explosives and iron filings.

He also put in a diagram of the trebuchet, a weapon for flinging missiles, and the description of a military rocket.

The largest cannon of its time was built by Mehmet II, and was used in the siege of Constantinople. It weighed 18 tons, and was 17 feet long, 2 feet in diameter, and the barrel was 10 feet long. This cannon was able to fire a cannonball up to a mile.

The Offering of an Heir

"And why should we not rely upon Allah while He has guided us to our good ways. And we will surely be patient against whatever harm you should cause us. And those who want to put their trust should put their trust in Allah." {The Qur'an, 14:12}

Obedience takes courage, loyalty, commitment, forbearance, generosity, sacrifice, and asceticism. It takes recognizing the natural law of everything Allah has created, and a willingness to obey. If Stephen Hawking's theory about the 'Big Bang' is correct, and many agree with him, then there are some fascinating facts orbiting around.

(1) One second after the 'Big Bang' temperatures fell to a mere ten thousand million degrees.

(2) One hundred seconds after the 'Big Bang', the temperature dropped to one thousand million degrees.

(3) An average galaxy is one hundred billion stars, and there are over one billion galaxies, with the universe still expanding.

(4) The Universe would not exist if there was a decrease in the expansion rate one second after the 'Big Bang' by only one part in one hundred thousand million million.

(5) If there is a change in the gravitational force by one part in ten to the forty, nothing would exist (What is one part in ten to the forty? Well, if you stretch a tape measure across the entire known Universe, and set gravity at one inch anywhere on the tape measure, if it moves one inch one way or another, we don't exist).

(6) Our DNA contains the information of a thousand complete sets of the *Encyclopedia Brittanica*.

(7) Time/space is an envelope we exist in.

(8) There can be no disobedience to the laws of nature.

Man is the only creature created (besides the DJinn) who was given free will to turn away from his Creator. To choose obedience is to find peace with the natural laws of Allah.

Here is a dutiful companion in complete submission…

Umm Sulaym bint Milhan Al-Ansariyyah

Quote: *"Know that the reality of freedom is the perfection of servitude."* – Al-Qushayri

Umm Sulaym started her life as a Muslim when she was married to someone not willing to accept the call of Islam. Her husband tried his best to make her give up her new religion, asking her if she had gone mad, but she stood her ground and refused to turn away from the truth. When she started teaching their son, Anas, about the oneness of Allah, her husband threatened to leave. He finally left her and went to Syria and she received news that he had been killed.

After her husband's death, she wanted to give a precious gift to the Prophet (pbuh), but she was poor. She thought of the most important and priceless thing to her, so she took her son, who was only ten at the time, and gave him to the Prophet (pbuh) to serve him. She only asked that the Prophet (pbuh) make supplication for Anas to gain the best knowledge. From the supplications of the Prophet (pbuh), he was well known throughout his life as one of the most knowledgeable companions.

Obedience

Umm Sulaym decided she would not accept any proposal of marriage until Anas was older and had come of age.

When Anas came into his own, Umm Sulaym began to soften to the idea of marriage. There was a formidable young man in Madina named Abu Talhah, who was a leader of his tribe. He became interested in Umm Sulaym, and was attracted to her integrity and courage. He proposed marriage to her, and offered her an enormous dowry, but unimpressed, she told him it would be impossible because she was a Muslim and he was not. He insisted and pushed harder, but she finally asked him if he worshipped things that grew out of the ground. He replied in the affirmative and she then asked him if he wasn't ashamed of that. He was speechless at that, and said, "If I become Muslim, then would you marry me?" She smiled and said, "Yes, my dowry from you would be your acceptance of Islam." He agreed to this, and when he arrived at the home of the Prophet (pbuh), he said, "Here is Abu Talhah with the light of Islam in his eyes!"

They married soon after that and had a son, but the child fell ill one day. Abu Talhah was so worried, he would ask about the boy when he arrived home, and would not be quieted until he had seen him. One day, not long afterwards, the boy died just before Abu Talhah came home. With the patience of one firm in her faith, Umm Sulaym waited for her husband to come home, and when he asked about their son, she replied, "He is better than before." Abu Talhah was pleased with this and so she fed him dinner, and then they shared intimate time together. Afterwards, she asked him, "If someone is entrusted with something of another's, and then they come to claim it, should it be given to them?" Her husband answered, "Of course, and happily!" "Well," she replied tearfully, "Allah took back the son He had entrusted to us."

When Abu Talhah went to the Prophet (pbuh) the next morning to tell this story, he (pbuh) made *du'a* for them to have their night together blessed, and Umm Sulaym became pregnant with a righteous son. After his birth, she would not breast feed him until she had sent Anas with the baby and some dates to the Prophet (pbuh) so he could bless him. The Prophet (pbuh) chewed some of the date and rubbed some on the lips of the newborn, and asked Allah to bless him. He named him Abdullah, and this child grew up to have seven children, all of whom memorized the Quran.

Umm Sulaym saw many miracles from the Prophet (pbuh) in her time, one of which involved the blessing of her meager food one night, which then fed over eighty people.

Umm Sulaym went to battle with the men and gave them comfort, water, and dressing for their wounds. She and Aisha would fill water skins and sling them over their backs, refreshing the fighters as they moved among them. Umm Sulaym used to carry a small spear or dagger with her there, and when she was asked why, she answered in a brave spirit, "If any enemy soldier comes near me, I will slit his belly!"

This brought forth a very joyous laugh from the Prophet (pbuh).

Her brother, Haram, along with his brother, Sulaim, were fighting near the Prophet (pbuh), and died right before his (pbuh) eyes. He always had a soft spot for Umm Sulaym after that. Her perfect submission to obedience brought a blinding luminary to the world in the form of her righteous son, Anas. He lived to be one hundred and three, and had eighty children, many of whom became learned scholars in Islam. She left her legacy in Islamic history by bowing her head to her Lord in all matters. Her son, Anas, related that the Prophet (pbuh) said, "When I entered Paradise, I heard footsteps and a noise. I asked who it was, and they told me it was Umm Sulaym."

~~~

From the characteristics of the companions was they would not neglect good deeds whenever they were presented, and if not presented, they would seek them out.

Hasan al-Basri (ra) would do good deeds excessively saying, "For the likes of me there are not optional deeds, but the optional deeds are for one who has finished his obligatory deeds."

Salman al-Farsee (ra) would say, "The one who does optional deeds excessively and does not complete the obligatory actions is like a trader who lost his capital, but he still seeks profit."

Bringing It Forward to Today

If we sit and think about this story, and how Umm Sulaym handled the death of her child, the depth of her patience feels almost out of our grasp. She overrode her own grief to make her husband comfortable. She piled good deed upon good deed, until it made her a stairway to Paradise. We need to remember that even if we increase our good deeds and do not become tired of them, we still cannot thank Allah for even one of His favors on us. The blessings and beauty, as we see from this story, is in the trying…

Unearthing Hidden Jewels

Did You Know?

A Muslim woman named Fatima Al-Fihri built a university in Fez, Morocco in 859 that is still in use today. It is the world's oldest active university, and it is called 'Al-Qarawiyyin'.

Her father, husband, and sister died, leaving her a vast fortune. She wanted to do something for the sake of Islam, so she bought some land near her home, and decided she would build a mosque and school for the sake of Allah. She paid for it herself with *halal* money, and her stipulation was that every ounce of building material for the mosque/university must come from her land. This noble and blessed complex sprung up out of the earth beneath it.

She also decided to fast every day until it was finished out of gratitude to Allah, and the building took two years to finish.

It was a well-thought-out project with herb gardens inside the mosque and a well in the middle that was dug as soon as construction started so the workers and any passersby could benefit from its cool, sweet water. It is still there today.

The university had 8,000 students by the 14th century, some of the more famous ones being Ibn Khaldun, Ibn Al-Arabi, Pope Sylvester II, and Maimonides, a Jewish physician and philosopher.

The women of Islam have made their mark on this world in ways not imagined.

Sources

Sources

QURA'N SECTION

Ali, A. Yusuf: The *Meaning of the Holy Qur'an,* amana publications Beltsville, Maryland, 2009

Malik, MFA: *English Translation of the Meaning of al-Quran*, Texas, The Institute of Islamic Knowledge, 2001

http://www.quran.com

BRINGING IT FORWARD SECTION

Mujahid, Abdul-Malik: *Gems and Jewels: Wise sayings, interesting events, and moral lessons from the Islamic History,* Darussalamsalam

QUOTES

Al-Asamm, A: *Jumuah Magazine*, Volume 22, Issue 12, 2010

Shafi'i,: *Jumuah Magazine*, Volume 24, Issue 8, 2012

Al-Jawzi, I: *Jumuah Magazine*, Volume 24, Issue 4, March 2012

Al-Qushayri: *Jumuah Magazine*, Volume 25, Issue 4, 2013

Al-Khattab, U: *Jumuah Magazine*, Volume 25, Issue 6, 2013

Al-Baqir, M: *Jumuah Magazine*, Volume 25, Issue 6, 2013

Al-Qayyim: *Jumuah Magazine*, Volume 25, Issue 8, 2013

Unknown: *Jumuah Magazine*, Volume 24, Issue 7, 2012

Al-Khattab, U: *Jumuah Magazine*, Volume 25, Issue 7, May 2013

Al-Ghazali: *Jumuah Magazine*, Volume 25, Issue 5, March 2013

Quotes: http://dailybenefits.abdurrahman.org/tag/asceticism/

Quotes – Web

Quotes: http://dailybenefits.abdurrahman.org/tag/asceticism/

http://www.goodreads.com/quotes/tag/islam?page=2

http://www.ezsoftech.com/stories/mis15.asp

http://politicalquotes.org/node/59871#sthash.68QlO4r5.dpuf

http://www.spreadkindness.org/tools/kindness-quotes

http://www.brainyquote.com/quotes/quotes/c/charlesdic163892.html

COMPANIONS

Al-Basha, AR: *Portraits from the Lives of the Companions of the Prophet Muhammad* (pbuh), Volume I, Virginia, Institute of Islamic and Arabic Science in America, 1993

Khairabadi, M: *Devoted Companions Part I*, Pakistan, Islamic Publications, LTD, 1979

Khairbadi, M: *Devoted Companions Part II*, Pakistan, Islamic Publications, LTD, 1979

Ahmad, AB: Bilal bin Rabah, *The Mu'adhdhin* (caller to prayer), Houston, Darussalam, 2001

Tabaa', Asma: (Translanted by Sawsan Tarabishy), *Stars in the Prophet's Orbit,* self- published

Sources

OBEDIENCE

http://www.islamswomen.com/articles/umm_sulaim.php

http://idealmuslimah.com/personalities/sahaabiyaat/872-umm-sulaym-bint-milhan

GENEROSITY

http://sjpaderborn.wordpress.com/2012/05/27/who-was-rufayda-al-aslamiya-the-first-muslim-female-nurse-given-tributes

http://www.islam4theworld.net/sahabah/abdurrahman_bn_aur_R.htm

http://www.sunnah.org/history/Sahaba/ikrimah.html

http://www.inter-islam.org/Biographies/abdullahibnmasood.htm

http://www.sunnah.org/history/Sahaba/masud.html

COMMITMENT

Fatima:http://www.ummah.com/forum/showthread.php?251631-The-Sahabiyat-The-Female-Companions-of-the-Prophet-Muhammed

http://www.islamswomen.com/articles/fatimah_bint_muhammad.php

http://www.islamicweb.com/history/sahaba/bio.AT_TUFAYL_IBN_AMR_AD_DAWSI.htm

http://www.islamicweb.com/history/sahaba/bio.ABU_AYYUB_AL_ANSARI.htm

http://www.sunnah.org/history/Sahaba/salman.html

SACRIFICE

Nusaibah: Source: *Great Women of Islam*-Darussalam Publications

http://en.wikipedia.org/wiki/Nusaybah_bint_Ka'ab

209

Mus'ab: http://www.ummah.com/forum/showthread.php?291967-Mus-%91ab-bin-%91Umair-(Allah-be-pleased-with-him)

http://www.onislam.net/english/reading-islam/my-journey-to-islam/historical-biographies/431450.html

Amr ibn Al-Jamuh http://sunnahonline.com/library/history-of-islam/301-amr-ibn-al-jamuh

http://www.sunnah.org/history/Sahaba/jamuh.html

Jafar: http://www.sunnah.org/history/Sahaba/jafar.html

FORBEARANCE

Umm: Source: *Great Women of Islam* -Darussalam Publications (Umm Salamah)

Abu Hurairah: www.qurannsunnahresearch.com/english/images/pdf/abu_hurairah.pdf

Translated by Gamal M. Hegazi from *Men around the Prophet* by Khalid M. Khalid

http://en.wikipedia.org/wiki/Abu_Hurairah

Zayd Al-Khair: http://en.wikipedia.org/wiki/Zayd_al-Khayr

LOYALTY

http://www.islamswomen.com/articles/khadijah_bint_khuwaylid.php

http://wikiislam.net/wiki/Khadijah_bint_Khuwaylid

http://www.wisemuslimwomen.org/muslimwomen/bio/khadijah_bint_khuwaylid/

Hamza: http://www.al-islam.org/restatement-history-islam-and-muslims-sayyid-ali-ashgar-razwy/hamza-accepts-islam

Sources

http://www.ummah.com/forum/showthread.php?227547-Hamza-Ibn-Abdul-Muttalib-Lion-Of-Islam

Abu Ubaydah: http://www.sunnah.org/history/Sahaba/ubaydah.html

http://www.inter-islam.org/Biographies/AbuUbaidahJarrah.html

Thumamah bin Uthal: http://www.sunnah.org/history/Sahaba/uthal.html

http://en.wikipedia.org/wiki/Thumamah_ibn_Uthal

Asceticism

http://www.wisemuslimwomen.org/muslimwomen/bio/aisha_bint_abu_bakr/

http://www.islamicweb.com/history/sahaba/bio.aishah_bint_abiI_bakar.htm

http://muslimmatters.org/2013/02/08/ismail-kamdar-life-of-aishah-bint-abi-bakr/

http://www.beautifulislam.net/sahabah/aishah_bint_bakr.htm

Manuscript of "A Speck of God" Loretta J. Poisson

http://www.sunnah.org/history/Sahaba/rumi.html

http://www.sunnah.org/history/Sahaba/said.html

http://en.wikipedia.org/wiki/Said_ibn_Aamir_al-Jumahi

http://www.sunnah.org/history/Sahaba/abudhar.html

Courage

Khawlah bint al-azwar:
    http://www.siddiqi.org/khawla/khawla_bint_alazwar.htm

http://mosaicofmuslimwomen.wordpress.com/2012/01/09/then-khawla-bint-al-azwar-the-black-knight/

Abdullah b. Hudhafah as-Sahmi: http://www.sunnah.org/history/Sahaba/sahmi.html

http://www.missionislam.com/knowledge/books/compprophet.pdf

Abdullah ibn Umm Maktum: http://www.islamforlife.co.uk/sahabah.htm

http://www.sunnah.org/history/Sahaba/maktum.html

http://islamicthinkers.com/welcome/?p=413

FROM THE CHARACTER SECTION

Fareed, A: From the Characteristics of the Salaf, United Kingdom, Jam'iat Ihyaa' Minhaaj Al-Sunnah, 1996

DID YOU KNOW SECTION

Dirks, Jerald, *Muslims in American History, A Forgotten Legacy*, Maryland, amana publications, 2006

National Geographic Kids: *1001 Inventions & Awesome Facts from Muslim Civilization*, Washington D.C., National Geographic Society, 2012

Abdallah, O.F , *Famous Women in Islam*, CDs

"*1001 Inventions and the Library of Secrets,*" short feature film at www.1001inventions.com/libraryofsecrets

www.muslimheritage.com

Journey to Mecca, In the footsteps of Ibn Battuta, A King AbdulAziz Public Library and King Faisal Center for Research and Islamic Studies, Cosmic Picture/AK Films Production, 2009, Imax film

Sources

Tibet, *Jumuah Magazine*, Volume 24, Issue 4, 1433 H

Did You Know? Web

en.wikipedia.org/wiki/University_of_al-Qarawiyyin

http://stage1.whyislam.org/social-values-in-islam/fatima-al-fihri-founder-of-worlds-very-first-university/

http://thecorner.wordpress.com/2006/11/28/the-prophets-sword/

http://www.academia.edu/4250078/The_Story_of_Hajj_Ali_and_the_U.S._Camel_Calvary_Corps

http://lostislamichistory.com/columbus-was-not-the-first-to-cross-the-atlantic/ (Mandinka Inscriptions)

http://mosaicofmuslimwomen.wordpress.com/2011/12/19/then-queen-zubaida-bint-jafar-al-mansour/

http://www.sciencemuseum.org.uk/broughttolife/people/albucasis.aspx (Zahrawi-surgery)

http://www.muslimheritage.com/article/abu-al-qasim-al-zahrawi-great-surgeon

Ibn al-Haitham : http://lostislamichistory.com/ibn-al-haytham-the-first-scientist/

http://en.wikipedia.org/wiki/List_of_English_words_of_Arabic_origin_(A-B)

http://www.zompist.com/arabic.html

http://ibnbattuta.berkeley.edu/

http://en.wikipedia.org/wiki/Ibn_Battuta

http://www.saudiaramcoworld.com/issue/199801/islam.on.the.roof.of.the.world.htm (Tibet)

Unearthing Hidden Jewels

http://www.muslimheritage.com/article/al-jazari-mechanical-genius

http://www.1001inventions.com/media/video/clock

http://www.maxvanberchem.org/en/scientific-activities/projets/?a=128 (world's fair 1893)

http://publishing.cdlib.org/ucpressebooks/view?docId=ft8x0nb62g&chunk.id=d0e1831&toc.id=d0e1234&brand=ucpress (world's fair 1893)

http://www.islam-guide.com/ch1-1-a.htm (fetus)

http://www.islam101.com/science/embryo.html (keith moore) and the fetus)

http://www.uh.edu/engines/epi1910.htm (finas and plane)

http://en.wikipedia.org/wiki/Abbas_Ibn_Firnas

http://www.whyislam.org/muslim-world/baghdad-libraries-house-of-wisdom/

http://www.muslimheritage.com/article/abbasids%E2%80%99-house-wisdom-baghdad

http://www.guyguitars.com/eng/handbook/BriefHistory.html

http://www.astrolabes.org/

http://www.ted.com/talks/tom_wujec_demos_the_13th_century_astrolabe?language=en

http://cse.ssl.berkeley.edu/AtHomeAstronomy/activity_07.html

http://mosaicofmuslimwomen.wordpress.com/2012/01/30/then-mariam-al-astrolabiya-al-ijliya-scientist-inventor/

http://womeninislam1.wordpress.com/2013/08/15/famous-muslim-woman-scientist-who-designed-and-constructed-astrolabes/

Sources

http://www.accessgenealogy.com/native/melungeon-genetic evidence.htm

http://weeklyview.net/2013/01/24/the-melungeon-story-part-3/
  Elvis and Abe

http://www.mrbreakfast.com/article.asp?articleid=26 (coffee)

] en.wikipedia.org/wiki/Ziryab

http://www.islamicspain.tv/Arts-and Science/flight_of_the_blackbird.htm

http://www.muslimheritage.com/topics/default.cfm?ArticleID=374

https://sites.google.com/site/caroluschess/medieval-history/ziryab

http://historyofislam.com/contents/the-post-mongol-period/shajarat-al-durr-queen-of-egypt/

http://addictedtoramadaning.blogspot.com/2012/07/ramadan-challenge-day-7-sultana.html

http://www.muslimphilosophy.com/sina/art/ibn%20Sina-REP.htm

http://en.wikipedia.org/wiki/Avicenna

http://www.wdl.org/en/item/7429/

http://www.princeton.edu/~achaney/tmve/wiki100k/docs/
  The_Book_of_Healing.html

http://ibnsinafoundation.org/

http://www.youtube.com/watch?v=2nznATCv05Y (renaissance)

http://whc.unesco.org/en/list/119/ (Timbuktu)

http://travel.nationalgeographic.com/travel/world-heritage/timbuktu/

http://www.flickr.com/photos/33427270@N05/ (Al Udar Al Karima)

http://addictedtoramadaning.blogspot.com/2012/07/ramadan-challenge-day-6-al-udar-al.html

215

http://www.guide2womenleaders.com/Yemen%20 Heads%20of%20State.htm

http://ngm.nationalgeographic.com/ngm/0507/feature2/ (Zheng He)

http://www.chinapage.com/zhenghe.html

http://www.china.org.cn/english/features/zhenhe/131897.htm

http://plus.maths.org/content/cracking-codes

http://www.henry-davis.com/MAPS/EMwebpages/219mono.html

http://www.clarklabs.org/about/More-About-Al-Idrisi.cfm

http://www.touregypt.net/featurestories/itulun.htm

http://www.onislam.net/english/health-and-science/faith-and-the-sciences/429558-medieval-islamic-hospitals-and-medical-schools.html?the_Sciences=

http://www.geocaching.com/geocache/GC3990Y_a-history-of-cryptography

http://en.wikipedia.org/wiki/Al-Kindi

http://lostislamichistory.com/mongols/

http://en.wikipedia.org/wiki/House_of_Wisdom

http://www.paperonline.org/history-of-paper

http://www.silk-road.com/artl/papermaking.shtml

http://asianhistory.about.com/od/asianinventions/a/ InventGunpowder.htm